John and Patricia MacArthur, New Zealand, 1988.

John MacArthur

Servant of the Word and Flock

Other biographies by the author:

The Forgotten Spurgeon
The Life of Arthur W. Pink
D. Martyn Lloyd-Jones: The First Forty Years
D. Martyn Lloyd-Jones: The Fight of Faith
   (The Two-Volume Authorized Biography)
Jonathan Edwards: A New Biography
The Life of John Murray
Wesley and Men Who Followed

John MacArthur

Servant of the Word and Flock

IAIN H. MURRAY

THE BANNER OF TRUTH TRUST

THE BANNER OF TRUTH TRUST

3 Murrayfield Road, Edinburgh EH12 6EL, UK
P.O. Box 621, Carlisle, PA 17013, USA

© Iain H. Murray 2011

ISBN-13: 978 1 84871 112 9

Typeset in 11/16 pt Galliard BT at
The Banner of Truth Trust, Edinburgh
Printed in the USA by
Versa Press, Inc.,
East Peoria, IL

To
The Elders, Staff, and Members of
Grace Community Church
with thankfulness for the grace given to them
to serve Christians across the world.

Contents

Illustrations

Foreword

*F*riendship with John MacArthur over the last dozen years has been one of the happiest surprises of my life. Surprise because we live on opposite sides of the world, and because, coming from somewhat different evangelical traditions, we might not seem to be natural fellow-labourers. It was shared convictions on great truths that brought us together, as they are bringing others committed to Scripture together across the world.

Writing a biography of Dr MacArthur never occurred to me until an event in 2009. Prior to that date the elders of his church asked me to preach on the fortieth anniversary of his ministry at Grace Community Church at Sun Valley, Los Angeles, which was being marked on Sunday, February 1, 2009. I sensed that some comment by me on the ministry we were commemorating would be appropriate, but how to address that subject was not at first clear to me. Believing as we do that the pulpit on the Lord's Day is for preaching His Word, that possibility was excluded. I therefore settled for writing a biographical sketch as a short tribute.

Unknown to me, Phil Johnson and Mike Taylor (editors working for Grace to You and members of Grace Community Church) had a volume in preparation to mark the anniversary,

Truth Endures: Landmark Sermons by John MacArthur. This book was at the printers when my sketch arrived towards the end of 2008. Johnson and Taylor wrote, 'It came unexpectedly after corrected proofs had already been sent to the printer.' They 'stopped the presses' and included my sixty pages of 'biographical sketch'. While I appreciated this kindness and honour, I was conscious that I had left too much unsaid, and that led to the book now in the reader's hands. It includes most of that original piece with a good deal more. My hope is to pass on to others the encouragement that I have found myself in the record of John MacArthur's life and ministry.

This is still little more than a 'sketch': a full portrait must await a later date and come from another hand. It is not the time for a full biography while a person's life is still in progress. John's ambition is to minister the Word of God to the end of his life; in his phrase, 'to die with his boots on'. His father was spared to serve until he passed ninety years of age; whether our friend lives to that age or not, he believes it is a duty to keep 'growing' as long as life lasts: 'People sometimes point out to me that what I've said on one tape doesn't agree with what I said on a later tape. My response to them is that I am growing. I did not know everything then, and I do not know everything now.' So, as he said on another occasion, 'You'll never be able to evaluate the ministry of John MacArthur until all the evidence is in.'

While I have not written these pages in conjunction with John, the aid of a number of people in his congregation has been indispensable. Especial thanks are due to Rick Holland, Phil Johnson, and Don Green. Mr Johnson's knowledge of unpublished source material is unique; I could not have written without it, and it is my hope that he will himself one day write on the ministry in which he has so largely shared. Staff members, Pat Rotisky and Catherine Curry, have been a great help to me, and numbers of others at Grace Community Church have encouraged us in various ways. The days which my wife and I have spent at the church, and at Grace to You, will ever be treasured memories. In a congregation where the blessing of God is known there will ever be affection between the people, and others find a ready welcome. So it has been for us at Sun Valley.

I am indebted to John MacArthur for the liberty to quote him as extensively as I do; and to Mrs Patricia MacArthur for her valued measure of input and for allowing the use of family photographs. Banner staff have given their customary best support in the production of this title, and my friends, Ian S. Barter and John R. de Witt, gave helpful comment on my draft. Jean, as ever, has kept everything running happily in our home, while I only looked after the computer.

IAIN H. MURRAY
Edinburgh,
August 2010

Introduction

WHAT IS AN EVANGELICAL LEADER?

*P*rized by John MacArthur is an old edition of John Foxe's *Acts and Monuments of these latter and perilous days* (1563), the book which first printed the story of William Tyndale, translator of the English Bible and martyred in 1536. Tyndale's enemy, Thomas More, complained of him that he was 'both nowhere and everywhere': 'nowhere' because few knew his actual location; 'everywhere' because his testimony was reaching all parts of the English-speaking nations. John MacArthur would never think of it, but the words suggest something of a parallel to me. Through hundreds of radio stations his voice is heard over a thousand times daily around the world; his books are to be found in thirty-five languages; yet the local scene where he spends the great part of his life is little known by most who read him or hear him broadcast. He is also 'nowhere and everywhere'.

The element of personal obscurity is of no concern to MacArthur. He stands in that genuine evangelical tradition which has no time for the creation of religious celebrities. When Paul says, 'Let a man so consider us, as servants of Christ and stewards of the mysteries of God', MacArthur understands him to be saying; 'Don't make anything out of me. I'm just a servant of Christ. I'm an under-rower, a third-level galley slave; I pull my oar, and that's what I'm supposed to do, nothing worthy of special attention.'[1]

Tyndale was 'a gospeller', or, as we would say, an evangelical. I use the term in its traditional meaning. In brief, an evangelical is a person who believes the 'three Rs': Ruin by the Fall, Redemption through Jesus Christ, and Regeneration by the Holy Spirit. It follows that an 'evangelical leader' is a person who stands out in the advancement and defence of those truths. The title does not necessarily imply success judged by numbers and immediate results. On that basis neither Paul nor Tyndale might qualify.

1. An evangelical leader is one who leads and guides the lives of others by the Scripture as the Word of God. He seeks to repudiate every other form of influence and pressure. His great concern is to teach Scripture accurately, and to see lives submitted to its authority.

2. An evangelical leader inspires the affection of followers because they learn Christ through him, and see something of Christ in him. They follow him because he follows Christ. And they love him because he loves them in Christ's name. 'The apostle Paul summarized the spirit of the true leader when he

---

[1] *Hard to Believe* (Nashville: Thomas Nelson, 2003), p. 46. An 'under-rower' is a favourite simile with MacArthur and he explains it further in *The Master's Plan* (Chicago: Moody, 1991), p. 39: 'There are several words in the Greek for servant, and Paul used the one that best conveyed the idea of a lowly servant (GK., *huperetes*, "an under-rower").' It was the name for the slaves on the lowest deck of a three-tiered ship propelled by oars.

wrote, "Imitate me, just as I also imitate Christ."[2] And what is to be imitated the Scriptures do not leave in doubt: 'Almost every time Scripture holds up Christ as our example to follow, the stress is on his humility.'[3]

3. An evangelical leader is a man prepared to be unpopular. From the days when Ahab said to Elijah, 'Are you he that troubles Israel?', faithfulness to Scripture will not bring the approval of the majority. Dr MacArthur says bluntly, 'You cannot be faithful and popular, so take your pick.' A quest for popularity is a very short-term thing. For an evangelical, 'success isn't measured in hours, or even centuries. Our focus is fixed on eternity.' Success 'is not prosperity, power, prominence, popularity, or any of the other worldly notions of success. Real success is doing the will of God regardless of the consequences.'[4]

4. An evangelical leader is one who is awake to the dangers of the times. Not every Christian has the distinction that was once given to the tribe of Issachar, 'The men of Issachar had understanding of the times, to know what Israel ought to do' (*1 Chron.* 12:32). There are periods in church history when the leaders have seriously mistaken the way in which the cause of Christ is to be carried forward. The signs of the times have been misread. A true evangelical leader is raised up to provide God-given direction.

5. An evangelical leader will not direct attention to himself. He personally owes everything to Jesus Christ. As a sinner he sees the need to live in a spirit of repentance all his days. He knows the contrast between what he is in himself and the mes-

---

[2] *Twelve Ordinary Men* (Nashville: Thomas Nelson, 2002), p. 44, in a chapter where MacArthur sets out what leadership means.

[3] *The Jesus You Can't Ignore* (Nashvile: Nelson, 2008), p. 205.

[4] *Ashamed of the Gospel* (Wheaton: Crossway, 1993), p. 29.

sage that he preaches: 'We have this treasure in earthen vessels, that the excellency of the power may be of God, and not of us' (*2 Cor.* 4:7). 'God chooses whom He chooses in order that He might receive the glory. He chooses weak instruments so that no one will attribute the power to human instruments rather than to God, who wields those instruments.'[5]

It follows that genuine spiritual leadership will lead others to the conclusion: 'Not unto us, O Lord, not unto us, but to Your name give glory, because of Your mercy, because of Your truth' (*Psa.* 115:1).

---

[5] *Twelve Ordinary Men,* p. 13.

1

Youth in California

*J*ohn Fullerton MacArthur Jr. was born in Los Angeles, California, on June 19, 1939. Rather inaccurately 'Junior' was often to remain appended to his name, for the truth is that many a 'John MacArthur' had gone before him. One of the MacArthur family by that name had emigrated from Glasgow, Scotland, to Canada in 1815. This immigrant's son and grandson were also 'John', and it was not until a fourth-generation member of the family line was born about 1885, and named Harry, that the Christian name changed.

Harry MacArthur, the grandfather of our subject, was working as a chief telegrapher on the Canadian Railways at Calgary, Alberta, when he became a Christian. His wife, Olivia Mary Fullerton, was the daughter of a Thomas Fullerton, who was minister of the Presbyterian Church of Charlottetown, Prince Edward Island, on the east coast of Canada.[1] Fullerton had come from Scotland where his father had also been a Presbyterian minister. There was thus Scottish ancestry on both sides of the marriage of Harry and Olivia.

[1] Thomas Fullerton was minister of St James Presbyterian Kirk in Charlottetown, 1893-1921, a ministry interrupted while he served in the Canadian army during the Boer War.

Harry and Olivia MacArthur moved south to Los Angeles while their only son, John, born in 1914, was still a boy. Perhaps it was the desire to preach that drew the parents to California, for Harry was to prepare for the gospel ministry at the Bible Institute of Los Angeles. His subsequent life-work was to include a pastorate in the city, much preaching for other pastors, and the setting up of a radio broadcast, 'Voice of Calvary', in 1942.

John ('Jack') MacArthur, the son of Harry, attended schools in Los Angeles and then studied at Eastern Baptist Seminary in Philadelphia. Influenced by his father's life and example, it was his early ambition to devote his life to preaching the Word of God, and indeed he was to do that almost every week from the time he was nineteen. His first pastorate was at Manchester Baptist Church, Los Angeles, and in the same city on June 25, 1937, he married Irene Adeline Dockendorf. The couple had met some years earlier when Irene was fourteen, the year of her conversion. Their son, John F. MacArthur, was born in 1939, as already noted. Our subject would thereafter be known to the family as 'Johnny'. The complete family was to include three daughters, all younger than John: Jeanette, Julie, and Jane. Johnny's earliest memories of home were not, however, of the city where he would spend his life. Soon after his birth his father joined the extension staff of Moody Bible Institute as an evangelist, and his early infancy was to be spent itinerating with his parents from place to place, including Chicago and Philadelphia. Of the latter city, and a brief school attendance, he was to retain a faint recollection.

Early in the 1940s Jack and Irene MacArthur were back in the greater Los Angeles area, for a short period at Eagle Rock Baptist Church. When Jack was called to Fountain Avenue

Baptist Church, Hollywood, in 1943, his father took over the work at Eagle Rock. Jack's work in Hollywood saw notable conversions, including those of Roy Rogers and Dale Evans, who became close personal friends.

1. Jack and Irene MacArthur, 1950s.

John MacArthur would look back on childhood as a time when he was 'loved, affirmed, encouraged and trusted'. The 'trusting' part was not always easy for his parents in his early years. As a child he was almost incurably inquisitive. On one occasion his curiosity even led him to slide down into a storm drain that he wished to explore. Not surprisingly, his mother at times resorted to tying him with a long rope to their clothes-line pole. When such measures were no longer possible, his adventurous nature could give his parents further surprises. Once about the age of seven or eight, and perhaps 'dared' by school friends, he stood at the intersection of roads near his home, directing cars as though he were 'a traffic cop'. This ended abruptly when a car he sought to stop happened to contain his father.

That was not the only time he felt some 'firm corporal correction'. Another 'correction' he was to remember had to do with his trial of swear words he had heard used by older boys. This was short-lived, for it led to his mouth being washed out with soap! 'To this day', he would say in later years, 'when I overhear someone else using vile language, I start to taste the soap!'

But in the most important area of his life John MacArthur's parents were spared the concerns of many Christian parents. He was never to remember a time when his faith was not real: 'I always knew I needed Jesus as my Saviour.' His Christian experience came slowly with his years; there was no sudden change and no spiritual rebellion. While he was still young his father would often take him with him on engagements. One such outing was for a week of meetings at the church of another pastor. While Jack MacArthur was otherwise engaged, John (now about ten) was left with the pastor's son and other boys. They drew the young visitor into an escapade that was new to him and which involved an element of vandalism. John's conscience was so smitten that he had no peace until he sat with his father on the steps of the church, and spoke of his need of God's forgiveness.

Jack MacArthur gave much time to his son, and was his chief mentor. Many years later John would recall:

> It was my father's preaching that made the greatest impact. You don't grow up a pastor's son without hearing a few thousand sermons—some more than once. While I may

have occasionally nodded off in the pew, much of what I heard stuck. In fact, a few of his sermons stand out clearly in my mind to this day. What I found as I watched—and what has most profoundly influenced me—was that my father's life rang true. His actions and his attitudes didn't change according to where he was or whom he was with. He lived by the same standard he encouraged his family and congregation to embrace, and by doing so, refused to give us an excuse to compromise. In a word, what he taught me was the value of *integrity*.

Until he was ten years old, John also knew the influence and heard the preaching of his grandfather, Harry MacArthur, who died of cancer on February 18, 1950. Not long before that event John had made a last visit to him with his father, and would ever remember him with admiration. In one of Harry MacArthur's last sermons, preached in December 1949, his subject had been 'Heavenly Records', with Job 16:19 as his text: 'And now, behold, my witness is in heaven, and my record is on high.' This was made available to all who attended the funeral, and in a Foreword to the publication, his son wrote, 'A dying man was preaching, a man who knew the record of his life was written, and that he was to stand soon in the presence of his Saviour.' In that sermon was the preacher's last testimony:

> First of all, I want it to be recorded that Harry MacArthur, a sinner, accepted Jesus Christ as his Saviour and was 'born again', and made a new creature in Christ Jesus. Some believe that one can be saved by joining a church, but we know from the Word of God that this is not so. I was a member of a church in good standing at least two years before I was saved or even interested in salvation . . . The

second entry I want recorded is the fact that I have and do, publicly confess Jesus Christ before men.

In the words that followed, Grandfather MacArthur showed he was a soul-winner to the last. The Foreword to the published sermon noted his humility in particular: 'He was a magnificent soldier of the cross, but he never knew it. He was first of all a preacher of the glorious gospel of Jesus Christ. He often said there were others who could preach it better, but they could never preach a better gospel.'

By 1950, the year of his grandfather's death, John's father had moved to First Baptist Church in the suburb of Downey. It was to gain the reputation of being the fastest-growing church in the denomination. In addition to this ministry, he carried on his father's weekly radio ministry of 'Voice of Calvary', adding a television broadcast in 1956.

More memorable to ten-year-old Johnny in 1950 was the coming of his widowed grandmother, 'Nannie' Fullerton MacArthur, to live with them. She was to stay for twenty-eight years. Although it was a squeeze for seven to live in the small Downey manse, Johnny accepted having his single bed in a room shared with his grandmother. In the company of his mother, grandmother, and three sisters, feminine influence would play its own part in his upbringing. Of his mother and the family upbringing he was to say:

Mom never worked a day outside the home. We were her life. The house was always clean and comfortable, and she would always be baking cookies or bread or making something special for us to eat. When I went to college near home, I could count on finding her there, cooking, reading, knitting (needles and yarn were always close by or in her hands). She made an immense impact on our family. Along with my father, she raised us four children in the nurture and admonition of the Lord. We all grew to know and love God.

Perhaps the most important choice my parents ever made in raising my sisters and me had little to do with us directly. It didn't concern where we went to school or how often we received discipline. It didn't hinge on when we went to bed or what we ate for dinner. The most important choice they made as parents was their commitment to pursue a godly marriage.

Close relationships marked the family life. 'This may seem hard to believe', John would say in later life of his parents, 'but I have never heard them say an unkind word to each other or argue in an angry manner. They seemed always to overlook each other's faults.'[2]

John's shared bedroom with his grandmother was to continue for two years until they moved to the Glendale district and a larger home. (By the time he was seventeen John reckoned he had lived in seventeen houses.) The reason for the move was his father's desire to establish a new church at Burbank, which he named MacArthur Memorial Church in memory of Harry MacArthur. The church name had soon to be changed to Calvary

---

[2] From MS of an interview that Phil Johnson did with John MacArthur in the late 1980s, headed 'What My Parents Did Right', some of which appeared in a book compiled by Gloria Gaither. On the same subject MacArthur said, 'I believe the chief ingredient in a fulfilled family is not the love parents direct at their children, but the love they have for each other. That is the most securing element for children.'

Bible Church, for it alarmed Jack MacArthur to find that some people imagined he had named it after himself!

Glendale and Burbank at this time were fast-developing communities at the eastern end of the San Fernando Valley, an area of some 240 square miles, in Los Angeles County, but separated from the denser population to the south by encircling hills and mountains. At the beginning of the century only a few thousand people lived in the temperate grasslands and scrub of 'the Valley', mainly employed with cattle and wheat farming. Water from the Los Angeles Aqueduct (1913) introduced citrus fruits, followed by a boom in industry during the Second World War, and sprawling ranches gave way to urbanisation. But with the population of the whole valley a little over a million in 1960, housing in such communities as Glendale did not have the density the family had known in Downey in the city to the south.

As a boy, John was not always healthy. He spent more time sick than is usual with children, and occasionally in hospital recovering from such things as rheumatic fever and pneumonia. By his mid-teen years, however, when he was at high school at Colter Academy, these health problems were over and he became distinguished in baseball, football, basketball, and sprinting. Indeed such activities were his absorbing interest and a professional sporting career was an attractive possibility. But his mother had prayed that her son would be a preacher, and from his early years John himself had known a call in that direction. It was with that expectation in view that his parents sent him to Bob Jones University in Greenville, South Carolina, in 1957.

John was not overly enthusiastic about his parents' choice for his university years. For one thing there were no intercollegiate

2. Football, John playing for Los Angeles Pacific College against California State University in Long Beach, California, Fall 1962. 'Eye-black' is grease applied to reduce sun glare.

athletics at Bob Jones; and for another a 'fundamentalist' environment, which urged 'third-degree separation' from other professing Christians, was unfamiliar to him. He was later to regard the time spent at Bob Jones as providing him with a view of Fundamentalism from the inside, and the experience served to lead him to a closer study of Scripture.

At the end of his first year at Bob Jones, John, bound for home, shared a car with five other students as they drove through Alabama. While they were proceeding at speed, the driver lost control; a door burst open as the car turned over, and John was thrown out. He was to land in a seated position on the asphalt road and slide for over a hundred yards. Nothing was broken but third degree friction burns took the flesh off his back, and embedded asphalt in what remained. One hand would be scarred for life. 'As I stood up on that highway, having never lost consciousness', he would later say, 'I committed my life to serving Christ. I told him I would no longer resist what he wanted me to do, which was to preach His Word.' Three painful months followed the initial hospital treatment, requiring the patient to lie on his stomach, and undergo skin grafts and other treatment. Life suddenly became very serious: 'I realized I was not in control of my future. I had survived something that should have killed me; God suddenly had my undivided attention.'

This was a great turning point. From this time the Christian ministry became the pole star of his life. One more year, 1958-59, was to follow at Bob Jones in South Carolina, and it was during this year that he preached his first 'sermon'. The location was a bus station in Spartanburg, South Carolina, where he had been instructed to preach and gather a crowd. It was not exactly the situation for a novice, as he quickly discovered:

> The sermon was terrible. I didn't know how to do it right. I went in there—had my Bible in my hand—and I walked in to this mostly empty bus depot. As I looked around at a motley bunch, I started preaching a gospel message. You could just see the people looking at me and saying, 'The poor kid! He looks intelligent. It's so sad; he must have some kind of disability.'
>
> And I thought, this doesn't make any sense at all. So I did it for about ten minutes, and then I went down the street where there was a high school dance beginning. I sat outside and gave the gospel to the kids as they went in and out. That's how I got my start preaching. It wasn't memorable, but I was eager to learn to preach, because I was determined to be ready whenever I was called on. I would go to rescue missions and military bases to preach

when I could. Over time, I learned how to connect with an audience.

During 1959 John learned that he would be able to continue his Bachelor's degree at Pacific College in Los Angeles, and this led to the decision for him to do his two final years at that institution. Back home, sports were now resumed and he excelled, especially in football. He was named in an All-America squad as half-back, and was subsequently solicited by several professional teams to determine his interest in a football career. But there was now a higher purpose in his view, and this was confirmed to him by an unexpected opportunity arising out of a football luncheon at which he received an award. When he used the occasion to speak of his faith in Christ, one of his hearers asked him if he would visit a seventeen-year-old girl named Polly whose spinal cord had recently been severed in an accident.

John went to the hospital to see the girl who would remain paralysed for life, and her first words to him were, 'I'd kill myself if I could. I have no reason to live.' 'Not knowing what else to do', he recalls, 'I started into a presentation of the gospel. "It's not what happens to your body that matters, Polly, it's what happens to your eternal soul. You're going to live forever somewhere. God can bring joy into your heart even now if the issue of your soul is taken care of. Would you like to hear about how that can happen?"'

Her heart was opened to listen. After prayer and conversations on several occasions, she was able to say, 'You know, John, in some ways I'm glad this accident happened. If it hadn't, I would never have met Jesus Christ.' This early experience in pastoral work had a profound influence on John himself. 'After that exposure to the power of the gospel, I thought, This is all I want for my life. Nothing else even comes close in significance.'[3]

---

[3] *Hard to Believe*, pp. 71-2. 'She became a follower of Christ and eventually met and married a wonderful Christian man.'

2

The Bible Takes First Place

*A*n enthusiastic young man once introduced himself to a
well-known Bible teacher with the words, 'Oh, Sir, I'd
give the world if I knew the Bible like you do.' The older man
looked him straight in the eye and replied, 'Good, because that
is what it will cost you.' In 1961, now twenty-two years old,
John MacArthur proceeded to Talbot Theological Seminary,
wanting to face that cost.

Talbot, situated at La Mirada, on the southern side of Los
Angeles, had about 125 students. John's father had urged it on
account of the reputation of its dean, Dr Charles L. Feinberg,
who before his conversion had studied to be a Jewish rabbi. He
was said to know more than thirty languages, including Dutch,
which he had taught himself in order to read Dutch Reformed
Theology.

Prior to this date, despite the example of his parents,
MacArthur's commitment to reading had been comparatively
small, a fact that came out when father and son together met
Feinberg at the seminary. Jack MacArthur opened the interview
with the words: 'This is my son Johnny, and I want you to make
him a Bible expositor.' 'Well, what has he been up to now?' the

dean responded. And John heard his father reply, 'He's basically a football player.' At this Feinberg looked quizzically over his glasses as though to say, 'Are you kidding me?'

Father wasn't kidding. As John later wrote of this point in his life:

> When I was in college I didn't want to read. I was a typical athletic guy who was usually outdoors, and I preferred not to be indoors reading. I arrived at seminary and had no choice. So I just began to read and, of course, it was all about what I wanted to know. I really fell in love with reading theology.[1]

One of MacArthur's great incentives at Talbot was his admiration for Dr Feinberg of whom he says:

> He read the Bible through four times every year. Needless to say, he was exceptional and intense. We were all rightfully in awe of him, and I loved him at the same time. He was a real model for me.

The dean became his chief mentor and to please him was now part of his life. It was the more painful, therefore, to receive from him one of the most memorable rebukes of his lifetime. All students had to preach at least twice in the seminary chapel, and as they did so members of the faculty sat behind them on the platform and filled in critique sheets. When MacArthur's turn came he was assigned to preach on 2 Samuel 7, the passage where the prophet Nathan's encouragement to David to build a temple was overruled by God. MacArthur took as his main theme the importance of not presuming on God, and, suppos-

---

[1] *Rediscovering Expository Preaching* (Dallas: Word, 1992), p. 336. His earlier lack of interest in reading cannot be taken in an absolute sense for he had graduated at Pacific College with the Bachelor's degree, composed of a major in Biblical Studies and a minor in New Testament Greek.

ing that he had preached well, he anticipated receiving the high opinion of Dr Feinberg at the end of the service. Instead the critique sheet the latter handed to him was blank apart from the words, 'You missed the whole point of the passage.' Later he had to enter his teacher's study, to find him shaking his head in disappointment as he exclaimed,

> How could you? How could you? The passage presents the Davidic Covenant culminating in the Messiah and His glorious kingdom—and you talked about 'not presuming on God' in our personal day-to-day choices.

The hearer of these words says it was 'the deepest single impression I ever received in seminary. I can still hear Dr Feinberg's heartfelt admonition ringing in my ears. If you don't have the meaning of Scripture, you do not have the Word of God at all.'[2]

A visiting lecturer to Talbot, who also helped MacArthur, was Ralph Keiper of Philadelphia, secretary to Donald G. Barnhouse and the primary editor of *Eternity*. John never met Barnhouse but read some of his writings. Among anecdotes of Barnhouse that he would later use, was the occasion when the famous preacher was interrupted by an admirer as he was reading his Bible on a plane flight. 'I wish I could know the Bible like you do', the stranger exclaimed. Barnhouse's response was to say, 'Well, you could start by putting down *Time* magazine and reading the Bible.' One of the lessons Keiper impressed on John was the value of illustrating the teaching of a passage not by anecdotes but by other incidents in Scripture. Part of

---

[2] From an address, 'Why I Still Preach the Bible after Forty Years of Ministry', delivered at the first 'Together for the Gospel' conference in 2006, and as put down on paper by Phil Johnson.

the charm of Keiper's personality lay in his humour and in that area he was also of help to John. John's father, hearing some of his son's first efforts in speaking, had impressed on him, 'The pulpit is no place for humour. You've got to get out of that.' While Keiper was equally against turning sermons into entertainment, John says he helped him 'to have a little bit of humour in my life.'

Sports still took some time while he was at Talbot, and he had a good friendship with Feinberg's son Paul, who was an outstanding athlete. John still had an approach to turn professional, but the pull was no longer what it had been in earlier years.

Before he began his last year at Talbot, there was another life-changing event. Patricia Sue Smith belonged to his father's church, where her father, Dale Smith, was superintendent of the Sunday School, and for two years John had taught the Bible class to which she belonged. Dale, and his wife Lorraine (née Robertson), had moved to Los Angeles from a farming background in Nebraska in about 1940. Patricia was the fourth in their family of four daughters and one son. It was through a relationship between her and John's oldest sister that he became aware of Patricia, who was often in the MacArthur home. At some point she became to him 'the cutest girl I ever saw', and the fact that she loved the Lord determined the matter. Perhaps Patricia's estimate of John was a little longer in its formation, but all was settled to their mutual joy when they were married in August 1963. A later MacArthur title would be dedicated to 'Dale and Lorraine Smith on their Fiftieth Anniversary,' with gratitude that they have given their lives to the Saviour and me their daughter.'[3]

[3] *The Ultimate Priority: Worship* (Chicago: Moody, 1983).

3. John marrying Patricia Sue Smith, August, 1963.

Student days ended at Talbot in 1964 when MacArthur graduated *magna cum laude,* and with the Charles Feinberg Award, 'Given in Honour of the Outstanding Graduate'. He was also touched to receive two heavy boxes from his favourite mentor. They were Feinberg's personal set of Keil and Delitzsch's *Biblical Commentary on the Old Testament,* given with the words, 'That's for you. Now you have no excuse!' That same year he was ordained to the Christian ministry at his father's church by the Independent Fundamental Churches of America, headquartered at Westchester, Illinois.

MacArthur's way forward was now uncertain. One possibility was studying for a doctorate at Claremont School of Theology. This was to be a cross-roads decision that would affect the rest of his life and is best told in his own words:

When I was considering completing a doctoral degree in theology, the representative of the graduate program at Claremont looked over my transcripts and concluded I had too much Bible and theology in my undergraduate and seminary work. So he gave me a list of two hundred books of preparatory reading before I could be admitted to the program. I checked out the list with someone who knew the various titles and learned that none of them contained anything but liberal theology and humanistic philosophy—they were full of profane old wives' fables passed off as scholarship! The college also required me to take a course called 'Jesus and the Cinema'. This involved watching contemporary movies and evaluating them according to whether they were antagonistic to or supportive of 'the Jesus ethic'. The divine Jesus had been reduced to an ethic! I met with the representative again and said, 'I just want you to know that I have spent all my life learning the truth, and I can't see any value in spending the next couple of years learning error.' I put the materials down on his desk and walked away.[4]

This was not a decision lightly taken. To qualify for the course he had spent two semesters at a college learning German. There was more involved in his withdrawal than he fully understood at the time. Historic Christianity in the mid-twentieth century was in general decline in the English-speaking world and for the very same reason as it was before the Reformation: preparation for the ministry was corrupted. 'In the universities', William

---

[4] *The Master's Plan* (Chicago: Moody, 1991), pp. 153-4.

Tyndale wrote in 1530,

> they have ordained that no man shall look on the Scripture, until he be noselled [nursed] in heathen learning eight or ten years, and armed with false principles; with which he is clean shut out of the understanding of Scripture.[5]

MacArthur was being made aware of the same danger. In his later words:

> The mark of theological scholarship in some circles is no longer how well a man knows the Bible but how well he understands the speculations of the secular academic establishment.

He refers to the testimony of a friend at 'a well-known seminary' who asked one of his professors whether a class on personal holiness would not be appropriate for candidates for the ministry. The reply was, 'That wouldn't have any academic credibility.'

Looking back on his early years, MacArthur was to say:

> I am grateful to God that since the beginning of my training my mind has been filled with the truth of God. My mind is not a battleground of indecision about what is true and what is false, over things which 'minister questions rather than godly edifying' (*1 Tim.* 1:4).[6]

Had it been otherwise his ministry would never have been what it became. As a young man he had learned what Samuel Rutherford meant when he wrote, 'I may be a bookman, and [yet] be an idiot and a stark fool in Christ's way.'

In the years between his leaving Talbot in 1964 and 1969 MacArthur had no clear sense of direction. His father wanted

---

[5] *The Practice of Prelates,* repr., in *The Works of William Tyndale* (Edinburgh: Banner of Truth, 2010) vol. 2, p. 291.
[6] *The Master's Plan,* p. 153.

him to assist him at the Burbank church, and he did this for two years. But as Jack MacArthur was to maintain the church's pulpit ministry there was little opportunity for him to preach there. In 1965 John was also Assistant Professor at Los Angeles Baptist College. The next year Talbot Seminary invited him to act as an extension speaker and representative for them; the intention was evidently to show what the seminary could do for young men. He accepted and for the next three years it provided opportunities to preach in all kinds of venues, including Youth for Christ and Campus Crusade meetings, with conferences and camps for young people, especially in the summer. Sometimes this meant speaking up to thirty-five times a month.

The farthest from home for these engagements were successive visits to Mississippi. John Perkins, a black Christian from that State, had come to know John while temporarily in Los Angeles. He was also impressed by Jack MacArthur's radio and television ministry. When Perkins returned to the South it was to start a black church and a Voice of Christ Bible Institute in Mendenhall, Mississippi. For several years, John responded to Perkins's appeal for his help. There was a first Voice of Calvary Crusade in 1967, which, in the excitement of the times, Perkins described as 'the most significant ever to happen in Mississippi'. John shared in that first Crusade. It reached some 10,000 young black people from elementary school to college age, and brought home to him the greatness of their need for the gospel: 'At least ninety-five per cent of the people in the schools we visited knew nothing about a personal relationship with God.'

Social conditions in Mississippi in the 1960s showed John the impossibility of restricting aid to the black people only to the

4. John with John Perkins, at Mendenhall, Mississippi, 1967.

gospel message. Race tensions were running high. John Perkins had earlier seen his brother killed on the street by members of the white supremacy Ku Klux Klan. At Mendenhall John MacArthur always stayed in the Perkins home, and because of that known association he was refused meals at a white restaurant. In the near hopeless conditions in which black youth found themselves—life without meaning, purpose, or direction—he saw how they needed a vision to make life worthwhile. John reported in the columns of his father's *Voice of Calvary Bulletin* (March 1968):

> Young people need a goal. They need to feel they are getting somewhere and that their efforts are worthwhile. We encouraged them to go on with their schooling. We pointed out the relevancy of the gospel to the problems of today. We showed them how Christ can help them to be

better students, better neighbours, better football players and just generally better all-round people.

Inevitably black Christians such as Perkins had sympathy and connections with the Civil Rights Movement, although by no means all adherents to that Movement were Christians. Some—often white activists—discredited that cause by their manner of life. On one occasion John MacArthur was falsely identified with that element and taken to a police station for his supposed participation in the fostering of trouble. The charge was not sustained although he was made to pay a fine.

A second Crusade took place from March 31 to April 6, 1968. While it was being planned no one anticipated that the dates would coincide with a crisis in the Civil Rights Movement. On the night of April 4 John was in Jackson, Mississippi, talking with a group that included John Perkins and Charles Evers, the black Mayor of Fayetteville, whose brother was regarded as the first martyr of the Civil Rights Movement. John, the only white present, described himself later as a very young guy, who had grown to love these people and their culture. As they were discussing events a man burst into the room with the news, 'Martin Luther King has been assassinated'.

The group's reaction was to drive though the night to Memphis, the scene of the murder, and John went with them. As they left the house in Jackson he needed the care of his friends, lest he became a target for the anger of the black crowds already on the streets outside. At the motel in Memphis, where the Civil Rights leader had been shot only hours before, they found no police guard on the crime scene, and there was ready access to the landing stained with King's blood. Recalling that crucial time, John was to say: 'I actually went to the little building opposite the motel, went up on the second floor and, standing on a toilet, looked out of the window from which James Earl Ray had fired the shot that killed him.'

The experiences in Mississippi confirmed the truth to John that he already knew: the gospel alone could abolish the racial division, and he saw something of its power in the numbers of young people who were converted; some of them were to train for full-time Christian service. Of the 1967 Mississippi Crusade he wrote, 'I personally witnessed over 2,300 young people come forward to receive Christ. I watched them go step by step through the plan of salvation we put into their hands . . . each one represents a life committed to Jesus Christ.'

There was a significant maturing of MacArthur's thought during these itinerant years. When he left Seminary in 1964 he knew he was called to preach but the sphere of future service was by no means clear. Perhaps it would be the pastorate, or the work of an itinerant evangelist. Nor did he exclude the possibility of the mission field. Germany, in particular, interested him. Gradually it became clear to him that he was not to be an itinerant evangelist, 'with ten suits and ten sermons'. His experience had shown him that the *first* need of the churches was not evangelism:

> The overwhelming thing I saw was spiritual ignorance. Everywhere I went I saw insipid preaching devoid of biblical content. That really disturbed me. I constantly

reflected on the Hosea passage, 'My people are destroyed for lack of knowledge.'

This deepened his concern to give himself to an intense study of Scripture. In later life he would advise those who sought his aid over guidance, that God commonly guides His people by planting desires in them which He means to fulfil. Thus the promise, 'Delight yourself in the Lord; and He will give you the desires of your heart' (*Psa*. 37:4). This was certainly MacArthur's own experience.[7] His great desire was to know the Word of God and he saw that the time for this would only be possible when he was settled in one place. If his life was to be given to the Word of God, the pastorate was the calling for him. He also remembered his father's words that the preachers who left their mark on history 'stayed in one place for a long time'.

Patricia's thoughts coincided with those of her husband, for by now their family was arriving. Matt was born in August 1964, and Marcy two years later. Mark and Melinda were to follow in 1968 and 1973 before the family circle was complete. The place the family played was vital for MacArthur, 'I remember vividly when our eldest son was born, what it was like suddenly to feel the enormous weight of responsibility that comes with parenthood.'

During the late 1960s two well-established churches approached MacArthur with a view to his becoming their pastor; both decided that a man of twenty-seven or twenty-

---

[7] He did not recommend that guidance be found by first understanding one's own spiritual gifts. 'When I entered into the ministry, I didn't even understand what spiritual gifts were, and I was preaching and teaching and exercising my gifts before I knew what they were. It wasn't important that I analysed myself, but that I was obedient to the Holy Spirit and followed the desire He placed in my heart.'

eight was too young for their needs. Then an invitation is said
to have come in an unexpected way. At a summer camp at
Hume Lake in 1968, a group of high school youngsters from
Grace Community Church, Sun Valley, Los Angeles, were full
of enthusiasm at what they heard, and asked him, 'Would you
ever be our pastor?' Their wish was passed on to the officers
of their church with the result that MacArthur was invited to
preach in the fall of 1968. There is another account of how
John first came to be invited, and it has to be given weight
for it comes from Burt Michaelson, who was chairman of the
church's board of nine elders:

> One Sunday I heard Jack MacArthur's radio broadcast,
> and his son John was on it. So when the committee met,
> I brought his name up. Paul Sailhammer, who served on
> the committee, knew John. He called him and invited him
> to the church. Once John came and we had the chance
> to meet him and hear him, we never interviewed anyone
> else.

There is no reason why both of these accounts could not be
true. An invitation to visit and preach at Grace Community
Church was accepted, and John took for his subject a theme
much on his mind: Christians are weak because they do not
rightly understand their new identity in Christ. It is impossible
to live as God intends us to do unless we know who we are. He
took for his basis Romans chapters 6 and 7, spoke with liberty,
and must have entertained the hope that this congregation might
be the scene of his permanent work. If Patricia, who was with
him, shared that hope, it was dashed for her by the time he had
concluded his sermon. She met him with the words, 'Do you
know how long you spoke?' 'No', was John's reply, unconscious

of the time. 'It was an hour and fifteen minutes. Well, that's the end of that church. They'll never invite you back.' She was wrong. Grace Community Church was soon to invite him to come and preach to them all the time.

When settled in his own church, John MacArthur's father would be one of the first visitors to his pulpit. From him he had learned lessons that he would seek to practise in all the years that were to follow:

> My Dad used to tell me that a preacher ought to be ready to preach, pray, and die at a moment's notice. He made a great commitment in my life and had given me many things to pass on. His father had given him things to pass on. And what I have I have passed on. You have to take it, develop it, learn it, and pass it on to somebody else. This is a relay race, and we are all involved.[8]

5. Father and son, mid 1960s.

[8] *How to Study the Bible* (Chicago: Moody, 2009), p. 76.

3

The Early Ministry at Grace Community Church

*G*race Community Church, Sun Valley, called John
MacArthur in January 1969; he accepted and on February 9, 1969, began work in the congregation where he has
remained ever since.

Sun Valley is another district of the San Fernando Valley some
ten miles to the west of John's old family home at Glendale,
and approaching twenty miles north-west of downtown Los
Angeles.[1] The church had been formed in 1956 by Christians
from several denominations who were dissatisfied with what
they had found in the Hollywood area. With more open space,
at lower prices, still available in Sun Valley, the large block of
land obtained was more valuable than could have been recognized at the time. From the beginning to 1968 there had been
two pastors, Don Householder and Richard Elvee; the first a
Methodist and the second a Baptist. There was no denomina-
tional affiliation and the church's motto was the familiar words,

[1] On account of subsequent changes in boundaries, the present address of
the church is Sun Valley, but because the property is located on the dividing
line of two suburbs, it has sometimes been associated with Panorama City.

'In essentials unity; in non-essentials charity.' Within a five-year period both men had died of heart attacks on the church premises—perhaps a consideration that now entered into the call of a man of twenty-nine years.

'When I came to Grace Church, I didn't know much,' MacArthur was to say. But Charles Feinberg, and still more, his father, had given him strong foundation principles—the absolute authority of Scripture, the necessity of a true understanding of the gospel, and the danger of a false assurance of salvation. These notes were all prominent in his first sermon as pastor on February 9. The title was 'How to Play Church', and the text, 'Not every one that saith unto Me, Lord, Lord, shall enter into the kingdom of heaven . . . Many will say to Me in that day, Lord, Lord, have we not prophesied in Thy name . . . And then I will profess unto them, I never knew you, depart from Me' (*Matt.* 7:21-23).

It was a morning of pounding rain and the sermon had to be preached twice, for the church's building on Roscoe Boulevard in Sun Valley would not hold more than 300 and the membership was about 450. So Sunday services were 8.30 and 11 am, with an 'Evening Gospel Hour' at 7 pm. One of the original members of the church was Burton Michaelson, already mentioned, who explains that John MacArthur, and his family, were not entirely new to them. They had listened to Jack MacArthur's radio ministry and witnessed his son on the sports field when the young people of the church had taken on the youth from Calvary Bible Church. The one condition Burton remembered John stipulating when he accepted the call was that he be allowed thirty hours a week for study: 'We didn't understand that, but had confidence in him.'

The staff at Grace Community Church consisted of a secretary, a youth leader (also Sunday School superintendent), and Mrs Elvee, the widow of the previous pastor. The last named was clearly a major help. She 'mothered and protected him', as well as alerting him to items that needed his attention.

There had been blessing and growth in the church under its first pastors. A missionary concern was established, and there was some support for prayer meetings on Sundays and Wednesday evenings; the mid-week meeting also included a Bible study. Yet, as in all churches, the composition of the congregation was mixed, and the early days at Grace Church were not without their difficulties. At the outset there were some who did not like his first Sunday morning sermon on 'How to Play Church'.[2] 'As a result of that confrontational sermon several couples left the church, and we discovered that at least one elder was not a Christian.' That was not what the preacher wanted or intended: 'When I first arrived at Grace Church, my goal was to keep the people already there from leaving.'

Some things clearly needed changing. MacArthur made a start with proposals for the Sunday School:

> When I first came to Grace Church, I had a new idea about how to run the Sunday School. I wrote out my idea and presented it to the Education Committee. They unanimously turned it down. They said, 'Who are you, kid? We've been here longer than you.'

This incident contributed to a lesson that would guide his whole future ministry. 'I wasted a lot of energy when I was young trying to create concepts and programs to get everyone

---

[2] Published in *Truth Endures: Landmark Sermons by John MacArthur* (Los Angeles: Grace to You, 2009).

conforming into a slot.' He learned that life is more important than organization, and life is the result of inner attitudes.[3] So the first need was for hearts moved by God through Scripture, not for new methods or programs:

> The goal of a pastor and the leaders of a church should be to generate proper spiritual attitudes in the hearts of the people. They can't just say, 'You need to do this, and you need to do that.' They must generate the spiritual attitudes that will motivate the people to right behaviour . . . If the right kind of spiritual attitudes are present in a church, the structure will take care of itself, because Spirit-controlled people are going to do Spirit-led things.[4]

This lesson underscored the place of the pulpit. As God uses the Word preached, other things are bound to happen. This lay behind MacArthur's early commitment to expository preaching. Within a month of his settlement he took up verse-by-verse teaching from the opening chapters of Romans. Then he moved on to Ephesians 1, where the teaching on the believer's position in Christ provided a new foundation in the thinking of many.

One effect of God-anointed preaching is that a congregation will not remain simply listeners. Wherever there is real benefit from the Word of God there will be people moved to love and reach out to others. In a healthy church community Christian activity will be spontaneous. This is what happened at Sun Valley. There came a deepening spirit of zeal, enthusiasm, and sacrifice. One couple even gave up a honeymoon to be able to

---

[3] 'In nearly thirty years of ministry at Grace Community Church I have learned that if the spiritual attitudes of the people are right—as a result of careful, long-term, biblical teaching—the church's organizational structure, form, and style become far less important.' *Pillars of Christian Character* (Wheaton: Crossway, 1998), p. 8.

[4] *The Master's Plan*, pp. 31-2.

give more largely to the work. 'Programs' for evangelism were unnecessary as Christians made it their everyday business to live lives pleasing to God. It was proved that 'A congregation that evangelizes 365 days a year is better than a church which has a week of "revival" meetings once a year.'

> The church should emphasize ministry for every individual believer. Church leadership shouldn't recruit their members to do something out of legal obligation that they are not really motivated or gifted to do. Rather, the leadership should develop its members along the lines that the Spirit has gifted them. Aggressive, active, ministering people make a successful church.[5]

> We didn't have many formal programs, but everyone was ministering his gifts. People were always calling the church and asking if they could visit someone in the hospital, if the nursery needed more helpers, if someone was needed to clean the restrooms and windows, if help was needed to evangelize, or if someone was needed to teach a class. Everyone made himself available.[6]

Those who organized themselves to meet for prayer were at the heart of this activity.

> Our church has been labelled in some circles as non-evangelistic . . . Do you know what brings most of these people to a saving knowledge of Christ? It is their personal contact with faithful Christians. People in our church witness to their neighbours, co-workers, other parents in Little League, friends at school, people in the markets, their doctors, their attorneys, and everyone they meet. And over the years the Lord has blessed that one-to-one evangelistic

---

[5] *The Master's Plan,* pp. 60, 109.
[6] Ibid., p. 40.

activity to bring more people to faith in Christ than any
service, program, or event we have ever sponsored.[7]

So Grace Community Church did not grow according to
some pre-arranged plan; rather it was as individuals spontaneously recognized opportunities and took them. In that way a
tape-recording ministry had its beginnings.

One of the first articles on the church in a national Christian
magazine drew special attention to this point under the title,
'The Church with Nine Hundred Ministers'. The author was
Lowell Sanders, writing in *Moody Monthly*, June 1972. Sanders
on visiting the church was struck by the way it was a congregation where 'the people do the work'. The thirty-two-year-old
pastor told him, 'As the people see needs in particular areas,
they come to us with suggestions as to what should be done.
And I say to them, "Go to it!" As a result', Sanders continued,
'eight hundred to nine hundred people are actively engaged in
some form of weekday activity that strengthens and enlarges the
ministry of Grace Church.' Numbers of conversions took place
through local witness, in such places as a McDonald's where
members held a Bible study. Hunger for instruction led to a
'Logos Study Center' at the church on Monday and Tuesday
evenings, where other men were the speakers. And five hundred
attended the Wednesday Prayer Meeting in the new church
auditorium which had opened that same year.

It might seem from Sanders' article that MacArthur played
a comparatively small role. He told Sanders, 'To study and to
teach is the beginning, middle, and end of my responsibility.'
But the visitor recognized how everything began with the pastor's own devotion to Scripture:

[7] *Ashamed of the Gospel,* pp. 184-5.

He spends five to six hours a day, four or five days a week, with his Bible and books. Although his office door is always open to parishioners and he has no secretary near at hand to protect him, his people respect his need for uninterrupted study.

In the words of a later observer, Phil Johnson, the distinguishing characteristic of the congregation at Sun Valley became 'a fervent passion to understand and obey the Word of God'. MacArthur's hope was that 'every Christian would be like a battery that joins with other believers and corporately increases the church's output'. The picture recalls Spurgeon's words: 'Great things are done by the Holy Spirit when a whole church is aroused to sacred energy: then there are hundreds of testimonies instead of one, and these strengthen each other.'

Within this context, the life of Grace Church began to develop characteristics too often missing in evangelical churches. For one thing, emphasis was laid on the family unit, with no special attention given to youth. No sanction was given to the idea that the youth should be harnessed to 'set the pace for the rest of the church'. Such a procedure, MacArthur believed, injures the younger generation by displacing the lead that should be given by older Christians, including their own parents.

> The early church found its energy in its mature saints. Today the church is deriving its energy from young people. We need the energy that young people have, but we also need the power that older believers have developed from long, obedient lives.[8]

This absence of emphasis on youth was far from inhibiting their attendance. Sanders noted 'a great number of young

[8] *The Master's Plan*, p. 34.

people' at the regular services of the church, and taking notes on the hour-long sermons.

No less out of step with much contemporary church practice has been the commitment to church discipline at Sun Valley. This was not the case at first, but a change here also came about through the pulpit ministry. When MacArthur was preaching on 1 Corinthians in the 1970s, the exposition of chapter 5 made the motive for church discipline, and its importance, clear to all. Out of that chapter came the truth that the evangelistic witness of a church cannot be authenticated without the godliness of her members; therefore sin in the membership must be taken very seriously. 'Church discipline is the key to the purity of the church, which in turn will enable us to reach the world.' This was a principle some were ready to challenge:

> When church discipline was first applied at Grace Church, a couple of pastors said to me, 'It won't work. The church will be wrecked. You can't have everyone looking out for other people's sins.' I said, 'The Bible says we are supposed to be accountable to one another. Let's just do it and see what God does.'[9]

MacArthur had an absence of church discipline in mind when he observed of his father's work, 'I saw things that worked for my father and things that hurt his ministry.' Certainly the absence of church discipline was very widespread at this period. Phil Johnson has written: 'Grace Church became one of the first significant fellowships in this country to emphasize a biblical pattern of consistent discipline as a crucial aspect of church life.' One purpose of discipline is the restoration of offenders, and at times the church has seen that hope fulfilled.

[9] Ibid., p. 48. See also Appendix 4, 'Elements of Church Discipline'.

There have also been occasions when prompt action prevented the need for formal action. One such case followed when MacArthur was informed by a distraught member that her husband had just left her to go to live with another woman. Her pastor obtained the other woman's name, looked up her phone number, and rang the house. It happened that the missing husband answered the phone himself. What followed is best in MacArthur's own words:

> I said, 'This is John from Grace Church. I'm calling in the name of Christ for you to move out of that woman's place before you sin against God, your wife, and your church.' He was shocked and said he would go right back to his wife. The next Sunday he came to me, embraced me, and said, 'Thank you! I didn't want to be there. I was tempted, and I thought no one would care about that.' He wasn't alienated by my rebuke. Rather he was brought back to the fellowship and obedience.

God is honoured by church discipline even when the outcome may not be remedial. Grace Church has to be one of the few congregations where an individual's sin (where there has been no repentance) is addressed publicly according to the New Testament direction, 'Them that sin rebuke before all, that others also may fear' (*1 Tim.* 5:20). I was present on one occasion when MacArthur spoke from the pulpit about a church member who had deserted his wife and refused all admonition. With tenderness and solemnity, John announced that the individual had been put out of the church; simultaneously he called upon the members to remember the need of the man and his family in prayer.

There have been cases of churches making all kinds of differences and disagreements matters for discipline while overlooking the duty of 'forgiving each other, just as God in Christ also has forgiven you' (*Eph.* 4:32). The use of discipline to address small offences is a contradiction of the gospel, and MacArthur's balanced teaching on the subject of forgiveness is a no less valuable part of his ministry.[10]

❈❈❈

When once asked by a reporter, 'Have you always been driven by a desire to build a large church?' MacArthur replied that he had no such desire: 'I said Jesus Christ said He would build His church.' Servants of Christ do no more than fulfil what Christ has given them to do:

> If one desires to be faithful to Christ and His Word, there is no technique or system that will guarantee a large church. The church is a supernatural work. I must ascribe our church's numerical and spiritual growth to the will of our sovereign God. We are content to focus on aggressive biblical ministry and leave it to the Lord to add to His church (*Acts* 2:47). Our task is to be faithful.[11]

It was from this standpoint that MacArthur would later assess the growth of Grace Church in the 1970s. But if Sanders reported him correctly, John's understanding of the growth they saw was not the same in 1972. In the article referred to above, he wrote:

> MacArthur believes that any pastor who places a similar emphasis on an in-depth yet practical preaching of the

---

[10] See *The Freedom and Power of Forgiveness* (Wheaton: Crossway, 1998), also chapter 10 in *Truth Matters* (Nashville: Nelson, 2004). He rightly opposes the teaching that in all cases forgiveness may be withheld where there is no acknowledgement of wrong-doing.

[11] See 'I Will Build My Church', chapter 9 in *Ashamed of the Gospel*.

Word, and who will help his people develop and use their spiritual gifts, will enjoy the same results.'

He would not speak in that way in later years when he saw more clearly how providential circumstances, in which he played no part, had prepared the way. The Vietnam War had brought widespread disillusion; new Bible translations were prompting new interest in Scripture; and a hippy culture was being widely touched by 'the Jesus Movement'. It was a time when numbers, both young and old, were looking for a new direction. His mature verdict was: 'We were dropped into the right place at the right time; we caught the wave of those events.' 'I must ascribe our church's numerical and spiritual growth to the will of our sovereign God.'

6. Map showing local Freeways and location of
Grace Community Church.

4

Threatening Reversals

*J*ohn MacArthur has described the characteristic of his early
years at Grace Church as 'a time of discovery and estab-
lishing the truth'. It was also a period of remarkable growth,
in which, for a time, the congregation seemed to double every
year. As already noted, in 1972 the original chapel had to be
replaced by another, capable of holding up to one thousand.
This building was, in turn, superseded in 1977 by the present
worship centre with a capacity of around 3,000. Even that
accommodation was not enough for the numbers attending
and two morning services were still necessary. At the evening
service the auditorium was again commonly filled. It was well
that the ground owned by the church was large, for it meant
the new buildings were additional to the old that were retained
for other purposes. In this way the one site gradually came to
house a whole series of buildings.

The tape ministry, begun spontaneously by Vern Lummus
in his spare time in 1969, reflected the same growth. From
an annual figure of 5,000 tapes produced in 1970, the figure
rose to 37,000 in 1973, by which time six men (in a voluntary

capacity) were needed to keep it running under the name 'Word of Grace'. The annual figure was over 110,000 in 1976.

The church growth would surely not have happened if the 'pastor-teacher' had not made the local church his priority. Even so, it was impossible for him to avoid other demands on his time. There were invitations to speak not only from other churches, but from a whole range of sources, such as day schools, Bible Colleges, police wives, fire brigade functions, ministers' retreats, missions to the Jews, and Bible and prophetic conferences. While such outside engagements in the early years were in his home state, by the later 1970s there were growing calls from places as far away as Chicago (the Moody Bible Institute), Miami and Texas. Counsel from his elders on such multiplied commitments was forthcoming, as a letter the preacher wrote to the Secretary of the American Board of Missions to the Jews, on January 11, 1978, indicates:

> I have recently been instructed by the elders and my doctor to change my schedule for this year. This has necessitated my changing several things, including about five speaking conferences. There are some I am bound to and cannot get out of, but aside from these I have cancelled all until summer.
>
> The elders have directed me to concentrate here and to go on a missions trip with the staff to Brazil just two weeks prior to your conference.

The Brazil meetings in São Paulo went ahead in the weeks of April 17-28, 1978, with his main addresses on 'The Priorities of the Ministry', and 'The Characteristics of an Effective Church'. It was the response that followed this visit which helped the leaders of Grace Community Church to recognize how the ministry in their midst could have an international aspect.

Another demand on MacArthur's time also developed in the 1970s, and it took a high place in his agenda. In 1972 there were nine young men in the congregation conscious of the call of God to become preachers. John would meet frequently with them for prayer and fellowship, and his personal prayer was that their number would be greatly multiplied. The formal theological training of these men, and of others who joined them, was conducted at Talbot Theological Seminary, with which John retained his relationship. In 1977 the Seminary awarded him the degree of Doctor of Divinity. Originally the students for the ministry at Grace Community Church had a round trip of eighty miles daily, in a church-owned Dodge van, to the Seminary at La Mirada.

How this arrangement changed as the number of students from Grace multiplied was reported in a news item in *Christianity Today* (Feb. 10, 1978), under the heading, 'Seminary Goes to Church': 'More than 6,000 people attend Grace Community Church in Panorama City, California, and ninety to one hundred people in this relatively young congregation are seminary students.' It went on to explain that, as increasing numbers of these students were travelling back and forth to Talbot Seminary, it had been agreed that an extension campus of Talbot should be established at Grace Church. 'Instead of taking young people out of the church for three or four years of seminary, Grace has moved this seminary campus in-house to give its young people on-the-job training.'

Additional faculty and staff were now employed to make the Talbot extension in Sun Valley possible, and the regular input and oversight from MacArthur continued. A magazine of the Talbot Seminary students, *The Tiger Tale,* dated November 1,

1979, had for its leader, 'MacArthur's Love for Pulpit—and for Talbot Students'. The article began:

> The speaker: Dr John MacArthur. The day: a Monday off. The audience: seventeen in number—considerably smaller than the thousands who hear him preach every Sunday. But the pastor-teacher of Grace Community Church believes the opportunity is well worth his time. His listeners are Talbot students who attend his weekly expository preaching class at the Seminary's Valley Extension Center.

It is certain that a spiritual advance never occurs without opposition. One surmises from the dedication in MacArthur's first publication that all was not smooth in his early years at Grace. His first publication, a 33-page booklet entitled, *Christians and Demons* (1973), carried the words, 'To my beloved fellow elders at Grace, whose strength and faith has already seen us victoriously through many battles.' In at least one incident in the church there was a forceful reminder of the real enemy to spiritual advance. The course of a service was interrupted one evening by a girl seemingly under demonic influence. She kicked and screamed with a voice that was not her own. It left MacArthur conscious that 'the battle is not against men'.

In the year 1979 varied forms of opposition from both outside and inside the church emerged. The opposition began on February 3, 1979, when the *Los Angeles Times* headed an article with the words, 'Woman's Place is at Home', and proceeded to condemn a sermon MacArthur had preached on January 21, from Titus 2:4-5, where Paul encourages 'young women . . . to

love their children, to be sensible, pure, workers at home'. The
newspaper claimed that the sermon had brought 'the firing of
five or six secretaries on the church staff'. The report was false.
What had happened was that, following the sermon, numbers
of women re-examined their priorities, and some who were
full or part-time church employees resigned in order to give
higher priority to their homes and children. The Board of Elders
endorsed the sermon, and stated that the desire of the church
was 'to employ only those people whose employment would
have no negative impact on these God-ordained priorities'.

In subsequent years, MacArthur would often summarize the
scriptural teaching on married women with such words as:

> Whether a woman works outside the home or not, God's
> primary calling for her is to manage the home. It is the
> most exalted place for a wife . . . far more crucial to the
> future of a woman's children than anything she might do
> in an outside job.[1]

From within the church problems also suddenly emerged
in that same year 1979. While the elders were supportive, and
the congregation flourishing, John had not noticed anything
untoward in the attitude of some of the additional pastoral
staff employed to support him. Perhaps a trait in his make-up,
noticed by a later associate pastor, is relevant: 'You were always
quick to believe the best about people—and the last to believe
anything negative—sometimes even to a fault.'[2] Trouble erupted
suddenly at a Tuesday morning staff meeting. MacArthur opened
the meeting, as he often did, by expressing his appreciation for
their help and friendship, only to be stopped dead by the words,

---

[1] 'Should a Wife be Employed Outside the Home?' in *Successful Christian
Parenting* (Nashville: Thomas Nelson, 1998), pp. 224-6.
[2] Tom Pennington, speaking in 2009.

'If you think we are your friends you have another think coming!' He then found that the speaker was part of a mutiny. The experience shocked and devastated him. It was not so much the personal criticism that hurt, but the realization that there was disloyalty to the ministry at the level of the leadership. Those he had taken to be his friends, whom he had personally mentored, were undermining him behind his back. Such experiences, sadly, are not unknown in Christian work.

On June 12, 1979, MacArthur wrote to Dr George Sweeting of Moody Bible Institute, expressing his regret that something of an emergency was preventing him speaking at an Institute Conference in Chicago at that time.

It is not clear whether this letter relates to repercussions from 'Black Tuesday' (as the incident above came to be called), or to other problems:

Dear George

I wanted to explain my telegram with a personal letter to explain a bit more thoroughly my absence. This past month has been a difficult time for us in terms of re-evaluating our staff. Our music director resigned to take on another position . . . In addition to that rather crucial situation, the elders found themselves in the midst of some rather traumatic changes in the direction and assignments of our staff which called for a series of morning and evening meetings during that very same week [as the Chicago conference]. They felt it was crucial that I be there to take part.

I feel badly about missing the conference because it's been such a special time in my life. I was torn as to my responsibilities in both places and felt the Lord leading me to make the commitment to be here at Grace, even though it perhaps caused some difficulty for you.

By this same summer of 1979 another issue had begun which continued to be threatening for years to come. A few years before this, Kenneth Nally, a university graduate and athlete, had professed faith in Christ and joined the church family. By this date he had become a seminary student in the Talbot extension in Sun Valley. It was now that a broken relationship with his girlfriend triggered a long-standing depressive tendency and, despite the counselling by members of the church staff, a crisis came when he unsuccessfully sought to end his life. Only at that point did MacArthur become involved, visiting the young man in hospital. For this care the father appeared grateful, but when the son left hospital a serious problem remained which brought father and son directly to talk with John.

It became clear that a strong conflict existed within the family, so much so that Ken did not want to return there. Mr Nally Sr was an Irish Roman Catholic and deeply resentful of Protestantism. To ease a critical and possibly dangerous situation, John offered to take Ken to his home for a while, with the promise to do all they could to help. This arrangement was accepted, but it had to end by March 26 when John left on a two-week first visit to Scotland. While he was away Ken Nally shot himself in the apartment of a friend.

This was a very heavy blow to MacArthur, who thought highly of Ken and took seriously the young man's belief that he was called to the gospel ministry. Inevitably the death caused more media attention, with the congregation investigated for information on any other suicides that had occurred under MacArthur's ministry. One newspaper quoted a woman who said, 'I can understand why that fellow killed himself. I went to that church once and three days later tried to kill myself!'

When this hostile publicity was dying down, on March 30, 1980, Mr Nally filed a suit of 'clergy malpractice' against MacArthur, and sought one million dollars in damages. There were three counts:

1. The church, John and others, counselled Ken Nally to read the Bible, pray, and listen to church tapes and counsellors, but 'prevented' him from seeking professional psychiatric help.

2. Negligence in the training of the church counsellors.

3. 'Outrageous conduct' in that Grace Church taught that Catholics were not Christians, exacerbating Ken's pre-existing depression and eventually driving him to suicide.

When this went to court the only count taken seriously was the allegation that Ken had been prevented from seeking professional help. A year and a half later, when the church supplied thirty-two depositions showing that the statement was untrue,[3] the court threw out all three counts and ordered the plaintiffs to pay court costs. But this ruling was not accepted and the case went to an appellate court, to be reviewed by three judges. By a two to one decision, they overturned the first court's decision, on the grounds of a new charge introduced under the count of 'outrageous conduct'. It was argued by the plaintiffs that MacArthur's church condoned suicide on the part of Christians, and thus encouraged Ken Nally to regard suicide as an acceptable way out of his depression.

Although the claim on the teaching at Grace Church was false,[4] it meant a re-trial in the original court, which took place

[3] Eight medical professionals had, in fact, treated Ken Nally, and there had been numerous referrals made by the pastors at Grace.

[4] The claim was based on a sentence spoken by an associate pastor at Grace, eighteen months after the suicide. Lawyer Sam Ericsson responded: 'The record shows that everybody—John, his wife, and all the defendants—told Ken time and again that only God determines your life span and that suicide is wrong.'

over four weeks in 1985. At its conclusion the judge dismissed the case, holding that the First Amendment to the US Constitution forbids imposing duties on clergy for church counselling. The court also found that the pastors of Grace Church had acted properly in the way they sought to help Ken. Yet this second acquittal was again overturned at a further appellate court hearing in 1987. The finale was not reached until November 1988 when the Supreme Court of California, at San Francisco, finally dismissed the case. By this time it had been widely reported in the national press. The *New York Times* gave a lengthy summary in its issue of November 24, 1988. The *Washington Post* (Nov. 26) wrote of the widespread relief in churches, and asked the question:

> What would the world be like if individuals who seek to help others by providing sympathy, advice, and encouragement—all without charge—had to start buying malpractice insurance . . . There is more than good sense involved in protecting churches from this kind of litigation. How can a court, consistent with the First Amendment, decide that it is wrong for a minister to suggest certain prayers? It is the essence of religious freedom for individuals to make religious choices without regard to the standards of the state, and for clergymen to offer such advice without fear of being hauled into court.

Through the eight years in which this contest continued it might have seemed as if Grace Church had the sword of Damocles hanging over it. Certainly the issue was critical, yet newspaper reporters who visited the church during the period were surprised to find services continuing without so much as a mention of the law suit. MacArthur could say:

We're just carrying on our normal church worship and teaching the Bible. Our people are also praying for the Nally family. We have a great concern for them spiritually and never want to do anything that might put up more barriers than are already there.

What was of first importance in his mind was how the church re-acted to the trial:

It goes back to James 1. We are church people. For some reason God has chosen to put us in this situation. We count it a joy. If we were suffering because of evil doing, it would be a reproach to us, but if we suffer for righteousness' sake, we count ourselves worthy to be identified with Christ.

John also saw several signs of the providence of God in what happened. The final verdict had vital consequences for the churches in securing them against unjust litigation; but had another church been the target for what was a first law case of its kind, the outcome could have been different. It so 'happened' that out of 350,000 churches in 1980 only one had a lawyer with professional malpractice defence experience on its staff, and that was Grace Community Church. The lawyer was Sam Ericsson. Before the case concluded, Ericsson became director of the Christian Legal Society's Center for Law and Religious Freedom in Washington, and along with other legal helpers, continued to provide as able counsel as could be found in the land. At the Supreme Court the oral argument for the defence was led by Rex Lee, a respected orator and senior partner in a Washington, DC, legal firm. The church saw the hand of God in the readiness of these able men to help.

MacArthur was once asked, 'Are there special difficulties you have had to surmount and overcome?' He responded, 'There's a lot of pain in the ministry', and then spoke of the legal battle they had passed through. He also referred to 'two or three other times' when he was tempted to leave the church, 'when even the prospect of digging ditches for a living had a certain appeal'. Perhaps he was momentarily forgetting the words of Campbell Morgan he liked to quote, 'If you have no opposition in the place you are serving, then you're serving in the wrong place.'

The trials I have sought to describe undoubtedly strengthened his understanding of the nature of the Christian warfare and of the only effective response. Of course, critical men and women do not know that they are being used by the powers of evil. The weapons those powers employ

> consist of lies of all kinds—elaborate lies, massive philosophical lies, evil lies that appeal to humanity's fallen sinfulness, lies that inflate human pride, and lies that closely resemble the truth. Our weapon is the simple truth of Christ as revealed in His Word.[5]

The threatening days of the 1979 period drove the preacher at Sun Valley closer to Scripture. The work of God always brings fruitfulness in the life of the messenger as well as with the message. While MacArthur was prepared for his ministry by the years of study, what God did afterwards, in humbling,

---

[5] *The Truth War: Fighting for Christianity in an Age of Deception* (Nashville: Nelson, 2007), p. 49.

refining and sanctifying him, was essential to his usefulness. It is quality of life that makes a preacher persuasive, and that is something which is never self-produced.[6] While the public record of MacArthur's ministry might look like a success story, as in the case of Spurgeon, there were many trials and disappointments behind the scenes; these were all necessary to make him what he became. In those trials he had the unfailing support of Patricia, his parents, and faithful elders of whom he would later say, 'Those elders exhibited a love and commitment to God's Word that helped stoke a fire that has burned brightly for forty years.'

Before we leave the 1970s reference must be made to the series of sermons, on the Sermon on the Mount, in which MacArthur was engaged in 1979. It was probably the most greatly used series of the first eleven years of his ministry, in his own judgment, 'a major turning point in the life of our church'. When they were later published, he wrote in the Preface that of all the series he had delivered 'this one has brought a seemingly greater sense of conviction, more self-examination, commitment, and conversion of the lost than any other'.[7]

One of the crucial sermons in that series was entitled 'Which Way to Heaven?' When it was recently reprinted, Phil Johnson, the editor, commented:

Just a few weeks after preaching this message, John MacArthur took his first extended vacation since his arrival at Grace Church—a summer-long sabbatical with his

---

[6] 'Paul's preaching was persuasive; but it was his life that won the hearts of people.' *Expository Preaching,* p. 345. 'A sanctified preacher, known as such to his people, is a powerful instrument when he opens the Word.'

[7] *Kingdom Living, Here and Now* (Chicago: Moody, 1980). This title was in a sixth printing by 1988, and was reprinted in 1998 as *Only Way to Happiness.*

family. This sermon was still ringing in the hearts of people in the church when John returned in mid-September. The message was instrumental in motivating several long-time casual attenders of the church to examine themselves, and respond to Christ with real rather than superficial faith for the first time. It has likewise been instrumental over the years in bringing dozens, perhaps hundreds, of people to Christ.[8]

That 'first extended vacation' in 1979, mentioned above, was to stand out in John's memory, as he wrote twenty years later:

I took a three-month sabbatical from the church I pastor in southern California, and we loaded our four children into a van and toured the country for the summer. As you might imagine, spending ninety sweltering days in a van with five other people was quite an adventure. Between bathroom stops, meal stops, and stops just to keep the peace, I wonder how we managed to travel beyond the boundaries of our neighbourhood.

But God was gracious, and we had a wonderful time. We covered a lot of ground that summer. We saw majestic sights like the Grand Canyon and Lake Geneva. We visited historic landmarks like Gettysburg, Ford's Theater, and Plymouth Rock.

As I look back on those three months on the road with my family, I'm amazed at what I remember most. While I certainly enjoyed the places we visited and the things we saw there, the historic structures and beautiful scenery don't represent the highlights. What clings tightest to my memory are moments I spent with my family—the conversations I enjoyed with Patricia, the opportunities I had to play with my children, or a meal we ate along the side of the road.

[8] *Truth Endures*, p. 104.

But there was also an important long-term lesson about which Dr MacArthur wrote on another occasion:

That vacation of twenty-five years ago ended up being important in shaping my ministry at Grace Community Church and at Grace to You. Back then, Grace to You was young and just starting to get its legs. I had written a few small books. We had been on radio for only two years and were heard on just a handful of stations. While the ministry was growing, it was still small. Yet I had no idea how far-reaching and in demand it had already become. The trip my family took helped show me.

Along the way I met people whose lives had been changed by the verse-by-verse teaching of God's Word they had received from messages on tape and radio. People were expressing how they were sustained in their spiritual walk by our ministry. One family drove from Florida to a conference I was speaking at in New York just so they could meet Patricia and me, and tell us how much the ministry meant to them.[9] One young pastor came up to me, his eyes a bit watery, and said, 'John, don't do anything different and don't let anything change, because so many of us are depending on this kind of teaching.' It wasn't culturally relevant sermons drawing people to our ministry—it was divine truth, honoured, studied, taught, and re-taught. The Lord has used those encounters to confirm that novelty was not necessary. I needed to continue teaching the powerful Word, reiterating sound doctrines from all the rich texts of Scripture. Because God's Word is timeless, dynamic, and fundamental to godly living. No one ever outgrows it or exhausts its immeasurable depth.

---

[9] The New York Conference was only one of a number interspersed among the travels.

5

Scripture and Preaching

*W*hen Christian leaders appear in history the tendency is to interpret their influence too exclusively in terms of their background. Certainly John MacArthur's upbringing was in churches of Fundamentalist outlook, and the two men who most influenced his youth, Charles Feinberg and his own father, were in sympathy with much that the term represented. The spiritual standard that his father had set him was to be before him for much longer than his youth and was to continue into the following century. Dr Jack MacArthur would preach at Grace Church from time to time, and a note to him from John, dated December 28, 1981, tells us what that friendship meant:

> Dad,
>
> Thanks for a great message. I believe we will really see some fruit from the power of that presentation. One man had brought a friend, who said he was convinced, for the first time, that Jesus was the Christ. The tape will also have specially good use with Jewish people.

I praise the Lord for you and Mom—and the special way God has used you to prepare and bless me.

Love, Johnny

As late as 1996 Jack MacArthur was still to be found as a visiting preacher in his son's pulpit. In May of that year, John wrote in a Grace to You letter,

A few nights ago, I had the joy of yielding the pulpit at my home church to a man who knows me better than perhaps any other, and who has been the single, most powerful influence on both my life and the course of my ministry.

The grey-haired gentleman who stood in my pulpit Sunday night is my father, and he delivered a bold, articulate message to our congregation and the graduating students of the Master's Seminary. Dad has been teaching the Bible and shepherding God's flock for more than sixty years.

Jack MacArthur's encouragement to his son took different forms. Referring to the example of his father's study habits, John wrote in 1997:

'He was—and still is—an insatiable reader, a non-stop studier, and a life-long learner committed to enlarging his mind with important, stimulating books. Even now it's not uncommon for him to send me a package in the mail—several books along with orders to read them and give a full report on what I think.'

The debt John owed to his father in this regard is noted in the dedication of his *Commentary on Hebrews* (1983),

With loving gratitude to my father, Dr Jack MacArthur, who gave me the legacy of loving books and challenged me by his example to make use of commentaries.

It has become fashionable in evangelical circles today to join in criticism of 'Fundamentalism'. Perhaps MacArthur's early association with that tradition is the reason why his name is surprisingly omitted in a number of reputedly evangelical dictionaries. But Fundamentalism in America cannot be so easily ignored. As a movement it came into being early in the twentieth century as the unbelief prevalent in mainline denominations caused Bible-believing Christians to form new groupings. For the most part it was a stand for essential gospel truths, such as the infallibility of Scripture, the Person of Christ as God, and the necessity of conversion through faith in His death as our substitute. Fundamentalism, as Gresham Machen understood it, included 'all those who definitely and polemically maintain a belief in supernatural Christianity as over against the Modernism of the present day'.[1] And because it sought to be biblical, Fundamentalism retained gospel preaching and evangelistic urgency when it was disappearing from many churches.

That Fundamentalism also had a downside is a subject to which I will return later. For the present I am concerned with the belief that stood firm in Fundamentalism when it wavered or was lost elsewhere, namely: What Scripture says, God says. MacArthur grew up in that assurance and it has governed his life as a preacher. Eric Alexander has written, 'The fundamental place of preaching in the church is simply a corollary of the

---

[1] J. Gresham Machen, *What is Christianity?* (Grand Rapids: Eerdmans, 1951), p. 244.

fundamental place of Scripture in the church.'² How this works out in practice is to be seen in many ways.

To a marked degree Scripture has controlled MacArthur's selection of priorities in the use of time. The responsibility of presenting biblical truth to others overshadows everything else.

> The real goal of ministry has always been to keep my opinions out of it as much as possible. I never want to be guilty of giving people the illusion that they have heard from God when in fact they have only heard from me.

This has meant that in his personal life he has kept to the strict discipline of making everything subservient to the study of Scripture. For forty or forty-five Sundays, through forty years, two new sermons have been prepared every week; in the early years it was three, as he also spoke at the church prayer meeting on Wednesday nights. During the 1970s speaking at the prayer meeting was delegated to others, but he was never to vary from his commitment to preaching morning and evening on Sundays.

The pattern of his week was to give the best of his time, from Tuesday to Friday, to preparation for preaching. In early years this meant some fifteen hours of work for each sermon; and he still may require from eight to ten hours. He has lived out his father's admonition, 'Don't go into the sacred desk [pulpit] unless you are fully prepared.' A high view of Scripture will always lead a preacher to the right priority. The apostolic example, 'We will give ourselves continually to prayer and ministry

---

² Eric J. Alexander, *Biblical Preaching: Basics of the Reformed Faith* (Phillipsburg, NJ: P&R, 2008), p. 7.

of the word' (*Acts* 6:4), is always followed when the churches are in their healthiest state.

As another exponent of that fact wrote in the nineteenth century, 'If a minister would give the pulpit its appropriate energy, he will make all his varied experience subservient to the duties of the sanctuary.'[3] In MacArthur's case this has meant, 'I use a system I call "planned neglect": I plan to neglect everything until my study is done.'[4]

But no faithful minister is going to study Scripture simply in order to speak to others:

> Even if I never preached another sermon, I would thank God every day of my life for the sanctifying grace that has come to me through the daily study of His precious Word. Pastors should study to know God, not just to make sermons. For me, the greatest joy of preaching comes, not in the final step, proclamation, but in the transformation of my own life.

In that transformation far more is involved than personal study. Referring to painful experiences already mentioned, MacArthur has said:

> I have learned to embrace failure and criticism as probably the most productive work of God in my life. I can exegete a passage, what I cannot do is to refine myself. I cannot crush my own pride. So there is a sense in which the best things that have happened to me have been the disappointments and the misrepresentations.

---

[3] Gardiner Spring, *The Power of the Pulpit* (repr. Edinburgh: Banner of Truth, 1986), p. 119.

[4] This should not be understood as meaning that MacArthur is a comparative hermit. There are numbers of other weekly duties, and his preaching and addresses are by no means confined to Sundays. The able associates and staff he has gathered round him are an indispensable part to making his routine possible.

While the work of God in preparing a preacher is much broader than his study, it is in the study, as MacArthur has said, that he is constantly thrown on God. More is to be done than the application of his mind to the text. Prayer is bound up with sermon preparation: the preacher needs the conviction that he has a message both from Scripture and from God. 'I seek His direction, thank Him for what I discover, plead for wisdom and insight, and desire that He enable me to live what I learn.'

The study is therefore both a sacred and an exciting place. As MacArthur said to a friend while he was preaching through the Gospel of Matthew:

> There are many days when I can hardly stand what I am discovering. It just overwhelms me. In every paragraph there is this incomparable Jesus Christ and He is just devastatingly powerful and glorious. It is a crushing experience to be exposed to Him, and yet it is the most exalting thing—to realize He has embraced me for all eternity! I would rather preach Christ than anything else. He is the most compelling subject in all the universe.

The authority of Scripture is no less evident in the way a preacher handles the Word of God in public. The nature of Scripture as revelation from God must control the manner in which it is taught. There is something seriously wrong when a preacher thinks he must not put Scripture at the forefront of his message lest his hearers are 'put off'. It is no less wrong when a man thinks the best way to gain a hearing is to sprinkle the message with appealing stories and humour. A man who cannot get attention without these things, MacArthur would say, does not know what it means to handle the sword of the Spirit.

This is not to say that stories have no place in his preaching, but when they occur they should have no prominence and occupy little time. 'He does not dilute his sermons with stories', was the appreciative comment of one regular hearer. From his student days at Talbot, MacArthur was convinced that the best illustrations to use are those taken from the Bible itself. To stay close to Scripture in everything is to rely on the highest authority. 'Stories have emotional impact, but they are lightweight compared with Scripture.'[5] His second source for stories and illustrations is church history and biography.

The vital thing is that nothing should be introduced into a sermon that can lessen the recognition of hearers that the words which the Holy Spirit teaches are in a category all of their own. 'If any man speak, let him speak as the oracles of God' (*1 Pet.* 4:11). Thus when questioned on the use of drama and visual aids in the pulpit, MacArthur replied:

> You have to believe that the power of God's Word will be more effective than any human drama or communication gimmick. Nothing is as dramatic as the explosion of truth on the mind of a believer through powerful preaching.[6]

It is also MacArthur's belief that if Scripture is to be taught accurately, this is usually best done by the consecutive and progressive teaching of a congregation through different parts of the Bible. As already mentioned, the 'expository' method has been

---

[5] 'I tell a story when it is appropriate, but this happens only rarely.' *Expository Preaching*, pp. 342-3. Similarly, while MacArthur does not eschew all humour in the pulpit, his gift in that area is not in regular use. Preaching is not entertainment. 'There is great need in the church today to cry instead of laugh. The frivolity, silliness, and foolishness that go on in the name of Christianity should themselves make us mourn.' *MacArthur New Testament Commentary: Matthew*, vol. 1 (Chicago: Moody, 1985), p. 158.

[6] *Expository Preaching*, p. 345.

his practice from the beginning of his ministry, when he took up the Epistles to the Romans, Ephesians, and 1 and 2 Peter.

It is sometimes asked where the vogue for 'expository preaching' resurfaced in the twentieth century. Some have traced it to Martyn Lloyd-Jones. MacArthur, however, was listening to his father treat Scripture in a consecutive way long before he ever read anything by Lloyd-Jones; and he tells us that the examples his father followed were G. Campbell Morgan (1863-1945) and W. A. Criswell (1909-2002). There was to be, however, a growing difference between the older, Morgan-type exposition and MacArthur's. In his case, as with Lloyd-Jones, the devotional thought is grounded on the bringing out of clear doctrinal principles. Exposition needs to lead hearers to doctrinal certainties. MacArthur's definition of a strong congregation is a congregation that has learned to 'speak with one voice on essential doctrinal matters'. A sermon without doctrine does not build strong Christians.[7]

At the same time MacArthur's ministry has shown that the consecutive method of preaching through a passage is not the only way to be faithful in preaching. And he notes that sometimes what is called 'exposition' is deserving of criticism: 'The thing that kills people in what is sometimes called expository preaching is randomly meandering through a passage.' A mere running commentary on a passage is not preaching. If a sermon is going to be in a real sense a message it should have a clear theme, a unity of thought. As MacArthur's books show, while all his sermons are text-based, they are by no means all

[7] He comments that those who only preach short sermons miss this point: 'I am convinced that biblical exposition requires at least forty minutes . . . Rarely does a man preaching twenty-five to thirty minutes do doctrinal exposition.' *Expository Preaching*, p. 339. He would not say this, however, without adding the caution that length is not the main feature of good preaching.

tied in sequence to one book or passage. He has used a wise variation.

Another consequence of a preacher holding a right view of Scripture is that it will negate all contemporary ideas of adjusting the message to suit the 'target audience'. MacArthur sees the modern evangelical insistence on 'relevance' as seriously misguided. 'Relevance' has often come to mean that the presentation of Christianity should be guided by what men and women perceive to be their needs today. And because the modern world is thought to be so different from everything that has gone before, all that is 'traditional' in the churches comes to be questioned as a hindrance to an up-to-date presentation of the message. So a change in the presentation of the message comes to be justified in terms of an alleged greater effectiveness. Consequently, it is believed that the recognition of 'generational differences' is very important. Churches have even been known to advertise themselves as 'not your grandmother's church'.[8] An exponent of church-growth, quoted by MacArthur, says: 'Those who want to minister effectively in this generation must remember to keep their tone "optimistic".' On which MacArthur comments:

> The typical presentation today starts exactly opposite where Paul started. He wrote of 'the wrath of God . . . against all ungodliness and unrighteousness of men'. But modern evangelism begins with 'God loves you and wants to make you happy' . . . Let me say that I minister to a

[8] David F. Wells, *The Courage to Be Protestant* (Grand Rapids: Eerdmans, 2008), p. 212. This book is a powerful indictment of how evangelicalism has been misled in this area. In my opinion it is one of the most significant books to be published in fifty years.

rather large group from the baby-boom generation, and I disagree with that writer's unwarranted generalization that they automatically tune out negative truth. The ones truly being saved certainly must and will accept the negative as motivation to repent.[9]

Of course, this criticism of the quest for 'relevance' does not mean that all that is old deserves to be preserved; within the boundaries of Scripture there is always room for changes in style or method; but any thinking that credits man with the ability to decide what is 'relevant' is actually supplanting the Word of God. God has declared man's real need and it does not change from age to age:

> Church history is strewn with examples of those who thought they could mould the message for their own time—but ended by corrupting the truth . . . If church history teaches us anything, it is that different times do not require different messages. Those who preach anything other than the unadulterated gospel forfeit the power of God in their ministries.[10]

> Nothing is wrong with the message . . . If they don't hear the truth, cool music won't help. If they don't see the light, power-point won't help. If they don't like the message, drama and video won't help. They're blind and dead. Our task is to go on preaching not ourselves, we carry a supernatural message of everlasting life.[11]

Behind the cry for relevance, commonly, is a wrong estimate of human nature. Man fundamentally is a product not of his times but of the Fall. While the changes in the world are external,

[9] *Ashamed of the Gospel,* p. 132.
[10] *Truth Matters,* p. 108.
[11] *Hard to Believe,* p. 49.

human nature is abiding. Thus men today are dominated by the same sins as were present in the nineteenth or any other century. What was fundamental to the empires of Assyria and Babylon is to be seen in the nations today. As Lloyd-Jones used to say, men today may now travel at four hundred miles an hour instead of four, but they do the same things when they reach their destination.

> What, in reality, is the precise difference between the pride which the modern man takes in his culture and sophistication and the pride of those men who, at the very dawn of history, tried to build the tower of Babel into heaven?[12]

Wherever Scripture controls preaching, it means there will be dependence on the power of God in addressing the conscience of man in sin. That is the real point of contact (*Rom.* 2:14-15). Faithful preaching means addressing 'every man's conscience in the sight of God' (*2 Cor.* 4:2).

---

[12] D. M. Lloyd-Jones, *Truth Unchanged, Unchanging* (London: Clarke, 1951), pp. 111-2.

6

The Rediscovery of Old Truth

I earlier mentioned a downside to Fundamentalism, and it is with reference to this that John MacArthur's ministry moved in a significantly different direction. Some historical background is necessary to follow this development. In the early twentieth century, when there was widespread defection from biblical Christianity, fundamentalist churches, their organizations and publishers, drew together with something of a fortress mentality. They stood apart from those outside.

It is true that the line of division was not as sharply drawn in all parts of Fundamentalism. George W. Dollar, Professor of Church History at Bob Jones University, depicted Talbot Seminary, and the leaders of the denomination in which MacArthur was ordained, as 'moderate Fundamentalists'. They were men, he thought, who lacked 'a war psychology'. MacArthur saw something of the difference between Dollar's position and his father's during his two years of study in South Carolina, and it did not appeal to him. Yet at that date he was not conscious of the mistake which had weakened the fundamentalist churches in general. Their withdrawal from the historic Protestant denominations had engendered an indifference to what had once been the heritage of those denominations. Fundamentalism gave little place to church history before the nineteenth century. It was as though there was nothing to be learned from the confessions of faith and the literary heritage of an older evangelicalism. For the majority of fundamentalists, the best-known edition of the Bible was the *Scofield Reference Bible* of 1909, and few suspected the comparative novelty of some of its notes.

Lewis Sperry Chafer (1871-1952), friend of C. I. Scofield (1843-1921), was a standard-bearer of Fundamentalism. Distinguished as a preacher and an author, he founded the influential Dallas Theological Seminary in 1924. When B. B. Warfield of Princeton reviewed one of Chafer's books in 1919, he judged that it contained 'two inconsistent systems of religion . . . The one is the product of the Protestant Reformation and knows no determining power in the religious life but the grace of God; the other comes straight from the laboratory of John Wesley.'[1]

What Warfield meant by these words, and how MacArthur became convinced that his evaluation was true, is crucial to understanding the major development in the latter's ministry. The issue concerned the question whether the number who come to eternal life is ultimately determined by the purpose of God or by the will of man. By his opposition to the doctrine of election, Wesley tilted the understanding of numbers of evangelicals away from what had been the confession of the Reformation and the Puritans. But if man possesses a fallen nature, at enmity to God and to spiritual things, how can a 'decision' by him to turn from death to life be the cause of conversion?

---

[1] *Princeton Theological Review,* April 1919, p. 322.

Charles G. Finney (1792-1875) carried the deviation much further than Wesley by teaching that man does not have a fallen *nature* at all. He taught that faith is fundamentally a human decision and that salvation is secured by the sinner's movement toward God and the gospel.[2] This belief was almost universally accepted in Fundamentalism, and it was compounded by an error that came from another quarter. The scheme of unfulfilled prophecy that became accepted in Fundamentalism was Dispensationalism. This scheme believed that Scripture is to be understood as distinguishing sharply between 'law' (Old Testament) and 'grace' (New Testament). Jesus taught 'the law' because the new dispensation of 'the church age' had not yet begun, but for us who now belong to a new dispensation, the law has no place. J. N. Darby, Scofield's chief mentor, taught that Christ's preaching to Jews—as in the Sermon on the Mount—was no guide for preachers today; Darby held it was a *different* message because the Jews lived in 'the kingdom age'. Christians are now in 'the church age' which began after the Jews rejected 'the kingdom'. Whereas in the 'kingdom age' the message was 'law', in the church age it is 'grace', and these two things, it was claimed, stand opposed to one another. The law requires 'works'; the gospel is all grace. So an omission of the law of God—the Ten Commandments—became endemic in evangelism, and the unforeseen consequences were vast. If sin is 'transgression of the law', and if it is 'by the law' that the real nature of sin becomes

---

[2] *Ashamed of the Gospel*, p. 158. See also the extended Appendix, 'Charles Finney and American Evangelical Pragmatism', pp. 227-35. The pervasiveness of this teaching in Fundamentalism is scarcely open to question. George W. Dollar wrote that 'Most Fundamentalists . . . would have refused to adopt any statement of the Five Points [of Calvinism].' *History of Fundamentalism*, p. 276.

known (*1 John* 3:4; *Rom.* 7:7), then inevitably, where this is omitted, the seriousness of what it means to be an unregenerate sinner is going to be lost. When that happens, instead of pressing for conviction of sin and the fear of God, evangelistic preaching gives the main attention to encouraging sinners to make 'a decision for Christ'. In other words, everything necessary for conversion is reduced to the human choice, with the time of conversion determined by man. Even the work of God in regeneration is made a consequence of man's decision.

Another result of the thinking that made the work of God dependent on the human will was that a 'revival' can be planned and announced weeks before it is supposed to take place, the term being understood simply as a series of evangelistic meetings where 'decisions' would be certain and counted by the response to 'an altar call'.

This understanding of evangelism was so strongly established in Fundamentalism that it was no easy thing for anyone to depart from it. In John MacArthur's case the first step to a different understanding occurred while he was in Mississippi before he ever settled at Grace Church. We have noted him above recording the conversion of over 2,300 whom he saw 'come forward to receive Christ'. But in the course of participating in these Mississippi Crusades he came to see that, while real conversions took place, to estimate their real number by counting those who made a public response, was no sure guide. Experience made it evident to him that effective speaking, and urgent appeals, could account for numbers responding. From that time on he dropped the so-called 'altar call' as a supposed means of giving the number of conversions.

More slowly, however, did he come to see the effects of the popular practice upon the churches. Under a heading 'A Personal Lesson', he has detailed three cases of people who had gone back on a Christian profession. They were men who were all, at one point, close friends. The first was

> a high school classmate and team-mate. He and I worked summers at his dad's car dealership. We spent a lot of other time together besides work and school, passing out tracts and witnessing in Pershing Square in downtown Los Angeles. He seemed for all the world to be on fire for Christ.

The second friend was co-captain with him in the college football team, who also taught Bible studies and was thinking about the pastorate. The third man actually trained with John at Talbot. Yet all three were to abandon the faith; one was to be convicted as a criminal, and another was to erect a Buddhist altar in his home.

At one time he might not have been dogmatic on how to understand this abandonment of faith, but more reflection was leading him to a strong conclusion. It was stimulated, in part, by an experience in his early ministry which followed his meeting with a stranger. On a cross-country flight he found himself sitting next to a man. When this individual noticed that MacArthur was reading a Bible, he introduced himself and put the surprising question, 'Excuse me, you wouldn't know how I could have a personal relationship with Jesus Christ, would you?' What followed I give in MacArthur's own words:

> Prospects like this do not approach me very often, so I did not want to lose this one! I said, 'Well, yes, you simply

believe in the Lord Jesus Christ and accept Him as your
Saviour.' I explained that Jesus died and rose again so that
we might have eternal life. I told him all he needed to do
was to receive Christ as his personal Saviour.

'I'd like to do that', he said. So I led him in a prayer, and
he asked the Lord to be his Saviour. Later that month I
baptized him. I was very excited about what had happened
and eager to follow him up in discipleship. After a short
time, however, he broke off contact with me. I recently
discovered he has no continuing interest in the things of
Christ.[3]

While such experiences contributed to John's change of mind,
it was Scripture which finally convinced him that there was
something fundamentally wrong with the popular evangelism.
I have already noted his preaching from the Gospel of Matthew,
and its chapters on the Sermon on the Mount. It was during
his seven-and-a-half years of studying and preaching from that
Gospel (begun in January 1978) that he was finally convinced
of the difference between Christ's presentation of the gospel and
much contemporary practice. According to that practice, it is
an easy thing to become a Christian. But this was not what he
found in the Gospel narratives. Jesus, instead of telling would-be
disciples that they had 'only' to believe in Him, so often took a
different course. The lesson came home to him particularly as
he worked though the Sermon on the Mount, with its insistence on the place of the law. It also shook the self-confidence
of numbers of his hearers.

The final confirmation for him was Christ's dealing with the
rich young ruler in Matthew 19. Here was 'a young man who
asks in the clearest possible terms how he can lay hold of eternal
life'. The answer was he had to forsake all that he had:

[3] *The Gospel According to Jesus* (Grand Rapids: Zondervan, 1988), p. 77.

Instead of taking him from where he was and getting him to make a 'decision', Jesus laid out terms to which he was unwilling to submit. In a sense, Jesus chased him off. What kind of evangelism is this? Jesus would have failed personal evangelism class in almost every Bible College or Seminary I know!

It was now settled in MacArthur's mind that the falling-away phenomenon related to the fact that people were treated as converts who had never been converted at all. It was not because they did not 'believe' the message they had heard; they did, but this 'faith', instead of changing their lives, had allowed them to settle in a delusion. The message itself had misled them:

> Unbelievers are told that if they invite Jesus into their hearts, accept Him as personal Saviour, or believe the facts of the gospel, that's all there is to it. The aftermath is appalling failure, as seen in the lives of multitudes who have professed faith in Christ with no consequent impact on their behaviour.[4]

By means of such teaching large numbers are in the churches who are not Christians and they do not know it. They have been given assurance that to have 'good feelings' about Jesus is enough to show they are born again. In contrast to this, MacArthur saw that it is not the church's role to give assurance: 'The Holy Spirit alone gives genuine assurance (*Rom.* 8:16). Don't usurp His role in someone's life. Don't let false assurance overrule His conviction work.'[5]

MacArthur was later to be accused of falling into the 'error' of the Puritans. While Puritan authors were not the decisive cause of the development of his thinking, some of them were certainly

---

[4] Ibid., p. 79.
[5] *Hard to Believe*, p. 96.

a help to him at this time. It was the thoroughness of their commitment to Scripture which especially appealed to him.

> There was a day when the great students of Scripture and theology were pastors. Puritan ministers, rather than being just good communicators, were first and foremost students of God's Word. They worked at understanding, interpreting, and applying the Word of God with precision and wisdom.[6]

Thomas Watson was one of the first of the older authors to gain his attention. Watson is quoted repeatedly in the first volume of *MacArthur's New Testament Commentary* (on Matthew, 1985), and called 'the great Puritan saint'. In another book, published in 1983, MacArthur wrote, 'One of the great experiences of my brief life has been to read *The Existence and Attributes of God* by Stephen Charnock.' Other Puritan authors to whom he refers include John Flavel, Richard Sibbes, and Richard Baxter.

Connected with the above reading was his admiration for the books by Martyn Lloyd-Jones. He never met the one-time minister of Westminster Chapel, London, who died in 1981, but he came to quote him more than any other twentieth-century author.[7] His copy of Lloyd-Jones' *Sermon on the Mount* was bought in 1977 and was heavily marked. Some of the Welsh preacher's convictions, however, were his own before he ever read them in that source. He had, for instance, declined to share in Dr Billy Graham's crusades in Los Angeles on account of the latter's willingness to direct enquirers to non-evangelical

---

[6] *The Master's Plan*, pp. 151-2.
[7] Another twentieth-century 'Puritan' whom he came to quote at times was A. W. Pink.

churches, including the Roman Catholic.[8] Also included in MacArthur's widening reading, at this period, were the biographies of such evangelicals as William Tyndale, Jonathan Edwards and Henry Martyn.

MacArthur has written of Fundamentalism moving apart in two directions after World War II:

> One wing, desperate for academic respectability, could not resist the pluralism of the modern age . . . Another wing of Fundamentalism moved in the opposite direction. They were keenly aware that an obsession with academic respectability had led their brethren to abandon the fundamentals. For that reason they distrusted scholarship or spurned it altogether. This right wing of the fundamentalist movement was relentlessly fragmented by militant separatism. Petty concerns often replaced serious doctrine as the matter for discussion and debate.[9]

But a still more significant development from Fundamentalism and Dispensationalism was in the direction where MacArthur himself was now to lead. That a breach was occurring ought to have been clear enough in 1980 when he published a small book on the Sermon on the Mount, significantly titled *Kingdom Living, Here and Now*.[10]

---

[8] Graham crusades were held on three occasion in Los Angeles and each time the use of Grace Community Church for connected purposes was requested. MacArthur valued Graham's gospel preaching, and said nothing publicly critical of the evangelist until the latter expressed his agreement with Robert Schuller in 1997.

[9] *Reckless Faith: When the Church Loses Its Will to Discern* (Wheaton: Crossway, 1994), pp. 95-6.

[10] In his Preface to the book, reprinted in 1998, he noted: 'To declare Jesus' Sermon on the Mount irrelevant to this age is to cut the heart out of our Lord's instructions to His people.'

He would come to speak of B. B. Warfield as 'the great Reformed theologian', and take his side over against that of Chafer in the Princeton professor's review already quoted:

> If Chafer and those who were influenced by him had interacted seriously with Warfield on these issues, perhaps twentieth-century American evangelicalism might have been spared a lot of confusion and false teaching.[11]

The development from Fundamentalism that MacArthur came to represent, while retaining strengths that initially belonged to that movement, reconnected with the older Christianity of the Reformed tradition. What this would mean, the following years were to tell.

---

[11] *The Gospel According to the Apostles* (Nashville: Word, 2000), p. 125 n.

7

The 1980s

*J*ohn MacArthur's ministry entered a major new phase in the late 1970s in a way that seemed accidental. While the tape ministry developed during the 1970s, the preacher had no plans to create a media organization. It was a letter that came to Grace Church one day in 1977 that was to change the situation. The writer, from Maryland on the other side of the States, expressed his thankfulness for a MacArthur sermon on Ephesians which had been broadcast by the radio station WRBS, Baltimore. The letter was a puzzle to the staff at Grace Church for they knew nothing of any such broadcast. An enquiry revealed that a listener to that station had simply offered a MacArthur cassette recording which had been put on air.

This unexpected indication of how the ministry could be multiplied on air led to Grace making a tentative beginning with one radio station for a daily thirty-minute broadcast of MacArthur sermons. Once again, it was the work of volunteers that made this possible. These broadcasts, under the title Grace to You, were soon to multiply. By 1981 they were being carried by more than one hundred stations across the United States, and were heard in at least eighty cities. Nor were the broadcasts to stop at the nation's boundaries. By 1983 they were heard in Puerto Rico, with other countries overseas soon to follow, such as Britain in 1988. Referring to the 'turning point' that radio brought to his ministry in 1978, John was later to comment:

> Preaching on Christian radio had generally been relegated to hour-long broadcasts usually heard at weekends. In the Lord's perfect timing, Grace to You hit the air waves at a time when believers across the country were starved of Bible teaching, and we helped pioneer a half-hour format for daily preaching and teaching that is now staple. Back in 1978, no one expected our radio experiment would eventually have eternal implications for God's people across the globe . . . Truly the opportunities we have today are greater than any era in the history of Christianity.

The radio preaching had two unforeseen repercussions. It led to an explosion of interest in the cassette-tape ministry. From the one hundred tapes prepared weekly in 1970, Word of Grace produced a million in the twelve-month period a year after the sermons went on air. Overseas centres for their duplication and distribution came into existence in India, Singapore, Hong Kong, and the Philippines.

Further, the hearing of the spoken word fuelled a demand for written material by the preacher. In October 1979 MacArthur began to write a monthly personal letter to Grace to You supporters, and from the next year a four or six-page newsletter began to be sent out.[1] It was also in 1980 that a series of *Bible Study Guides,* in booklet form, was initiated. These were put together from his sermons by a new member of staff, Mike

---

[1] The personal letter has continued to the present date; the newsletter terminated in 1989.

Taylor, and were immediately in demand. The first issues in 1980-82 included such subjects as the 'Christian's Armour', the 'Holy Spirit', the 'Church', 'Heaven', and 'How to Study the Bible'. Ultimately there were to be 187 items in this series.[2]

MacArthur has always seen the gift of committed men, such as Taylor, to Grace Church as fundamental to the larger ministry. It was at this point that another such man came to them who would exercise a still larger influence in the realm of literature. Phil Johnson's name has already been mentioned several times in these pages. Born in 1953, he had joined the staff of Moody Press as a manuscript editor after graduating from Moody Bible Institute. When MacArthur was in Chicago, speaking at Moody Bible Institute in 1977, Johnson heard him for the first time. He came to that meeting as a reluctant hearer and only the persistence of a friend had got him there. For one thing, the visiting preacher's name was unknown to him; and he had heard enough speakers already on 'Guidance'—the subject on which the man from California was advertised to speak. It only took one hearing for Johnson's indifference to turn to admiration.

When Johnson moved on to be an assistant pastor in St Petersburg, Florida, his appreciation of MacArthur was to deepen. Finding himself in a situation where evangelism was identified with 'easy-believism', with regard for a changed life as evidence of authentic conversion ignored, what he heard from MacArthur broadcasts from Tampa, Florida, was a lifeline.[3] He remembers:

---

[2] The editing of the *Study Guides* was largely the work of Mike Taylor (1952-2009) who was hired for that purpose in 1982, and was to take a key role in the literature side of the work. He was still a staff member at the time of his death. A graduate of Michigan State University, he had come to California seeking work in the film industry before conversion turned his life in a new direction.

[3] The radio station in Tampa was one of only three in the nation that carried

For almost every day I listened to Grace to You on the radio. I was hooked from day one, and especially appreciated John's stance on the Lordship controversy because that was an issue that had immediate practical ramifications in our church's ministry to young people, which was one of my responsibilities.

Contrary to the popular teaching, Johnson heard MacArthur insist that Christ cannot truly be received as Saviour, unless there is also submission to Him as Lord. The two men had not met personally in 1977, but when Johnson was invited to meet MacArthur he relished the opportunity. The invitation came from his former employers, Moody Press, who wanted to commit the Californian preacher to a long-term series of commentaries on the New Testament. The attention of the Press had been drawn to the way MacArthur was preaching through the Gospel of Matthew and the possibility of an extended series of volumes was seen. The editing of material delivered in the pulpit would require skilled help, and it was estimated the whole project would take a ten-year period. Johnson was, accordingly, one of the six potential editors whom the publisher brought together to meet with MacArthur in Chicago in August 1981. After the meeting, Johnson recalls,

> John, who is extremely cordial in settings like that, made it a point to speak to each editor individually. My first ever words to him were, 'I listen to Grace to You every day and love your teaching. And I think you need to write a book on the Lordship issue.' He instantly replied, 'I do plan to write a book on that subject! I even have a title in mind: *The Gospel According to Jesus*. What do you think?'

Johnson was at this point considering returning to Moody as

---

the Grace to You broadcast in 1979.

acquisitions editor. MacArthur, who was at that time a board member of the Institute, knew of that possibility and encouraged him with the words, 'I'll tell you what. If you come to Moody as acquisitions editor, I'll make *The Gospel According to Jesus* a Moody Press book.' The younger man did go back to Moody and his first official job was to issue a contract to John MacArthur for that book. The friendship between the two men developed and the outcome was an invitation to serve as an elder in Grace Church and as Executive Director of Grace to You. Thus Phil, with his wife, Darlene, and their two children (and a third son already on the way), moved to Sun Valley in March 1983. From that date Phil Johnson began to take a lead in all editorial matters and to become John's right hand in 'translating' material preached into readable form. Until this point MacArthur's books had been comparatively few, and Johnson's presence would have a marked consequence in the flow of the preacher's titles that now went to the press.

If there was any thought that had priority in MacArthur's mind in the 1980s, next to the ministry in his own congregation, it was the need to help preachers, and to see others raised up for that work. He would often state the principle: 'Nothing is more critical to the health of a church than the quality of its leadership.' That conviction lay behind his input into the students at the Talbot extension program at Grace. It meant much to him that he could write in 1980,

Our tape ministry sends more tapes to pastors than any other single group. God has answered our prayers in this way by allowing us to be a blessing to pastors in their local churches.

In May of that same year, 1980, a five-day Shepherds' Conference for pastors was convened in Sun Valley. Fewer than two hundred men were present, but for John, who presided, the venture was 'one of the greatest events here at Grace Church. It was a thrilling time for them—and for us. God has called us to assist pastors all over the world, as Christ uses them to build His church.'

Word on the value of the Shepherds' Conference spread quickly, with the result that it came to be held twice a year at Grace. The numbers soon increased. In December 1984 John could note, 'We have hosted thousands of pastors at nine conferences.'[4] Simultaneously there was a demand for John to speak to gatherings of pastors in many places. When he was invited to a conference for French-speaking pastors in Montreal, in September 1982, such was the response that it led to the opening of a Canadian branch of Grace to You three years later.

The kind of pastors' conferences that John wanted to encourage can be seen in this note he wrote on objectives:

1. Renew the flame of pastoral ministry. 2. Give them a greater desire for the ministry which they have received from God. 3. Help them to forget themselves so that they may exercise a more efficient ministry. 4. How to discern leadership within the church.

His headings for what he was to say at one of these conferences further shows his intention:

Humility and teachableness—Perseverance in the face of discouragement—Devotion and loyalty to God, not the

---

[4] The figure includes Shepherds' Conferences in other parts of the country as will be explained later.

church—It is God's church—Nourish a sense of thankfulness and satisfaction for what they already have.

The need to be addressed in these conferences was more than simply the giving of instruction. After all, books can serve that purpose. It was to encourage the vision of what it means to be a 'man of God', to prompt the pursuit of godliness (*eusebeia*), and to warn against things that make for an unsanctified preacher. Preachers *themselves* need to be preached to. When MacArthur spoke to them this is what they got in addresses that included such words as: 'Watch your heart. Watch your motives. Watch your desires. Watch your conduct. Watch your behaviour.'

At the same time, in all these conferences for pastors, MacArthur is careful not to give any impression that listening to him, or trying to follow Grace Community Church, can lead other men to success. He never presents a program that will 'work' anywhere; on the contrary he knows men are commonly in situations different from his own situation:

> There are faithful saints in churches all across the country who sense no matter how hard they work, no matter how faithful they are, their church still struggles, falters, veers off course, and loses ground. Pressure bears down on us from the world and from within our own walls. Spiritual growth comes slowly.

The years 1985-86 brought two major additions to John's ministry with respect to the education of youth. The first of these was entirely unsought. At this date the Los Angeles Baptist College, founded in 1927 for the training of undergraduates at university level, was experiencing difficulties, and offered their work and its site to MacArthur and Grace Community Church. This offer was taken up. Re-named The Master's College, with MacArthur as its President in 1985, the institution was to see its enrolment almost doubled the following year. The aim was, and continues to be, serious Christian discipleship along with academic excellence. Since then it has generally had about a thousand full-time students, along with night classes for hundreds of others. Many parents have had the happiness of seeing the aim of the college fulfilled in their young people.

The second addition was the result of a deliberate wish on the part of MacArthur and Grace Church. The Los Angeles Baptist College had originally offered theological training. It would seem strange for Grace Church to take the control of a liberal arts college, and yet have no ultimate responsibility for the Talbot theological extension on its own campus. The time seemed right not to renew theological training at the college, but to open a new seminary under the church's oversight in place of the extension program.[5] Thirty-six students already trained on the campus were now serving churches and the need for larger numbers was evident. The components of the Talbot extension thus became The Master's Seminary in 1986. It was a formality for the student body of ninety-five to transfer. The same faculty of three instructors also continued, senior among them being Dr Irvin A. Busenitz, who had been a Talbot teacher since 1974. He remains to the present time the Professor of Bible and Old Testament. MacArthur, whose leadership lay behind the whole

[5] MacArthur had been offered the presidency of Talbot Theological Seminary. But his acceptance was impossible, and would have involved him in items, such as the training of women students, with which he was not in agreement.

project, was President, and Dr Charles Smith was called from Grace Theological Seminary, Winona Lake, to be the Dean and the Vice President. Subsequently Dr Richard L. Mayhue, who was an associate with MacArthur at the church from 1980 to 1984, returned to Grace to join the faculty in 1989, becoming Dean and Senior Vice President.

In a Grace to You letter of September 1986, MacArthur wrote of the features that were his vision for the new seminary. They included:

1. A faculty committed to nurture, not just to lecture. 2. A commitment to small-group discipling relationships between students and faculty members. 3. A focus on high-quality personal, educational, and ministerial development. 4. The cultivation of an attitude of worship and spiritual devotion. 5. An expositional curriculum and ministry model. 6. An internship program that complements the student's program of study. 7. A program designed to culminate in ordination for ministry. 8. A placement ministry committed to assisting each graduate in the early years of ministry. 9. A positive outlook focusing on biblical certainties and God's grace rather than critical theories or reactions. 10. A chapel program carefully structured for specific spiritual goals related to Christian living and ministry. 11. The cultivation of a worldwide vision through involvement in evangelism and missions. 12. A discipling ministry available for each seminarian's wife and family. 13. Effective training in leadership attitudes and skills.

In all the expansion of the 1980s there were at least two dangers of which MacArthur was conscious. He was aware of how some preachers built para-church organizations which weakened rather than benefited the churches at large. Their high profile and apparent success drew people and resources that were needed elsewhere. MacArthur saw the purpose of both Word of Grace and Grace to You as service to churches, 'the main ministry should flow from them'. His desire was that 'our radio teaching not hinder, but strengthen every aspect of the service of pastors across the land'.

> Our role is not to supplant the local church's ministry, but rather to work alongside the church, providing another resource for those hungry for the truth of God's Word. Media ministries can never substitute for involvement in a biblical church, group Bible study, or interaction with a teacher.

MacArthur was outspokenly opposed to any thought that his radio or tape hearers should treat the church in Sun Valley as a substitute for a local church of their own. In all the information that went out from the Grace media agencies it is remarkable how very little is ever said of the congregation he was serving. He also taught the staff of Word of Grace and Grace to You not to imagine that his ministry had some indispensable place in the kingdom of God. Thus when on one occasion he was warned that one of the radio outlets might have to close down as the income received could not meet the funding required, his reply was, 'So what?'

The second danger in the expansion was that it would drain the attention MacArthur could give to his own congregation. If it had all come about only by human arrangement this would no doubt have happened. But, as already noted, each new development had seen the God-given provision of like-minded colleagues. John had elders and others beside him who understood very well that the whole work depended on keeping the preaching of the Word of God at the centre, and that meant relieving John of many other things. As he commented in 1986:

Their work behind the scenes frees me up from many of the day-to-day tasks I might otherwise be faced with, and that enables me to concentrate on the priorities of my family, study and teaching.

Well-wishers occasionally suggested an alternative role to him. Why did he not consider laying aside the local church commitment and simply serve the churches by radio and conferences in the wider fields which were open? To that possibility he was never drawn. Once asked by one of his young sons, 'Are you going to retire, Daddy?', the answer was, 'As the Lord permits, I hope to continue teaching God's Word and shepherding His flock until the day I go to be with Him.' His whole life was, and remains, bound up with the people at Sun Valley. He has never wavered in the conviction that the pastorate was the work God had given him. An article he wrote on 'Ten Reasons I am a Pastor' underlined why he put this calling first. The reasons included the following:

The church is the only institution Christ promised to build and bless . . . The corporate functions of the body all take place in the church . . . I can be consumed with study and communion with God. There's a public side to me that the congregation sees, but there's a private side to me that only God knows. While I might preach three hours a week, I study thirty. And those hours spent each week in God's presence are a high and holy privilege . . . I am directly responsible to God for the lives of the people He has given me to shepherd. As a radio teacher, I'm not as personally accountable for how people apply God's Word. But as the pastor-teacher of a congregation, I have a relationship with my people like that of a shepherd and his sheep. I watch over their souls as one 'who will give an account' (*Heb.* 13:17) . . . I share the joy of parents over the birth of a child, as well as the pain of children over the death of a mother or father. I help celebrate a wedding: I also offer comfort at a funeral . . . I feel loved, appreciated, needed, trusted, admired—all a result of being an instrument God has used in the spiritual progress of His people. I know my people pray for me and care deeply about me . . . The reward of being a pastor far surpasses any frustration I ever feel in the ministry. And so I say with the apostle Paul, 'I press on toward the goal for the prize of the upward call of God in Christ Jesus' (*Phil.* 3:14).[6]

The work in the congregation at Sun Valley, instead of being weakened by the additional agencies, was rather encouraged by them. The fact that all came under the oversight of their elders gave unity to the whole, and there was enthusiastic help from unpaid volunteers for Word of Grace and Grace to You. At this same period much was also going on at the church itself. A day school for children up to fourteen years of age was started in 1980. Aid for the mentally impaired and the handicapped was strengthened. Thirty missionaries had gone out from the church and were being supported. A thriving bookstore, The Book Shack, was open daily, for MacArthur believed in the ministry of books as an integral part of good teaching.

It was no part of the vision of the leadership at Sun Valley that a church may be a preaching centre, where individuals have no commitment to one another, and no oversight is exercised. In

---

[6] Published in *Masterpiece*, Nov. – Dec. 1990, pp. 2-3.

1984, when it was clear that too many people were in attendance without becoming members, teaching was specially directed to this subject. The result was 1,200 new members, and approximately three hundred baptisms.

In a December 1984 letter to 'Beloved partners in ministry' the pastor reflected on the growth of the work, and continued:

> I've grown spiritually in these last five years, and I trust you have too. It's good to be able to look into the past and see the hand of the Lord, and the marvellous way He works to conform us to the image of His Son. The external growth of this ministry is definitely encouraging, but it's the evidence of spiritual growth that means the most.

If this testimony had not been true for MacArthur, and he had relied on himself, the weight of ministry in the 1980s could have marked its end. He knew the work in which he was sharing was not his accomplishment. Martin Luther wrote to John von Staupitz in 1522 about the Reformation: 'Christ is doing this without us, of course, without the help of a human hand, solely through the Word.'[7]

If Luther's words seem an exaggeration let it be remembered that Luke described the advance of the gospel in similar terms when he wrote 'the word of God grew and multiplied' (*Acts* 12:24; 19:20). John could say:

> From the very beginning, I was convinced that Grace to You would only be used of God if we were continually faithful to the proclamation of the Scripture. I can promise that God will bless that, I can't promise that He'll bless anything else, but I know He will bless His Word.

---

[7] *Luther's Works*, vol. 49, '*Letters*' (Philadelphia: Fortress Press, 1972), p. 12.

7. John and Patricia with family, 1988: (left to right) Kelly (née Gallagher) and Matthew, Marcy, Melinda (kneeling below), and Mark.

8

Across the Pacific

Overseas there came a similar development. A first international office of Grace to You was established in Mumbai (Bombay), India, in 1981, and during that decade the ministry at Grace Church was to go on air in a widening circle of nations from Australia and South Africa, to the Philippines and the United Kingdom.

John MacArthur is not by temperament a traveller. As already mentioned, he was in Brazil in 1978. He made a first visit to Britain (Scotland) in 1979, but it was not until 1988, when he was forty-nine, that he toured a series of countries across the Pacific. It was prompted by news coming back through the tape and radio ministry. In a Grace to You letter (February 1986) MacArthur reported:

> Phil Johnson, Managing Director of Word of Grace, recently returned from a three-week trip to Asia, and he told me he learned of Christians who listen to Word of Grace tapes in several places we didn't even realize we were penetrating—in the remote provinces of the Philippines, in the slums of India, and even in an out-of-the-way place like North Borneo. It's exciting and awesome to think

that messages I preach from our church pulpit are being heard by people in parts of the world I will never be able to visit. At the same time, it is a powerful reminder of the weight of responsibility that God has placed on all of us who know the truth. If the message is biblical, it has no geographic or cultural bounds.

As the value of MacArthur making a visit to some of these far-off places became clear to him, and to the elders at Grace, a tour was planned for August and half of September 1988. Patricia and all the family were to go with him, so that in addition to preaching there would be some days for vacation. Not normally a journal keeper, John's sense of the potential importance of these weeks prompted him to keep a record of the whole period they were away.

For the first time the family stood on southern-hemisphere soil when their plane landed in Auckland, New Zealand, on Tuesday, August 2, 1988. It was the start of many new experiences. Driving on the left-hand side of winding roads, through green meadows, in sight of some of the land's seventy million sheep, and with Maori music and feasts in the evenings—these were things unknown in California. The first weekend was filled with engagements at Totara Springs and Auckland. Some five hundred to six hundred people assembled at the former for a conference where MacArthur spoke twice. The response of hearers pointed to the great need of the country: serious exposition of Scripture was uncommon and charismatic influence prevalent.

The next week took them to South Island, first to Shotover River Gorge, where they 'put on life jackets and got on a jet boat for the best thrills ever'! Then to Queenstown, before a five-hour trip to Milford Sound. John notes:

Only fifteen on the beautiful Volvo bus—breathtaking, magnificent scenery—nothing to match its grandeur. Cloudy, drizzly weather made for thousands of waterfalls . . . Milford Sound was beyond description—massive rock mountains rising straight out of the water to thousands of feet in height. The wonder of God's glorious mind and creative power was clear. The most spectacular scenery we have ever seen.

After a further conference at Christchurch, the MacArthurs flew to Australia, passing through Sydney ('brilliant weather, lovely city') to Adelaide. Sunday, August 14, was a full day in Adelaide, concluding with a service at the Town Hall attended by one thousand people at 7 pm. At that meeting Grace to You in Australia had a plentiful supply of books and literature that was speedily taken up. The preacher noted:

Amazed to see that so many had heard me preach on tape, or read books, particularly, *The Charismatics*. Australian churches are either liberal and dead or weak and charismatic, with few small exceptions. No strong leaders seem to be setting a national standard for strong doctrine, confrontational teaching and preaching. No one seems to be taking up the issues and confronting error—to become a clarifying voice and lead people to recognize the truth and hold the line for it. Charismatics and non-charismatics co-exist with seemingly no problems at present due to the weak, non-confrontive style of preaching. Mostly devotional, not doctrinal or even expository.

Two days later he was in Melbourne, and straight into a pastors' luncheon with 150 men; later a meeting with five hundred in Camberwell Town Hall. The interest in Grace to You literature was especially heartening. MacArthur noted in his journal:

My prayer is not unrealistic—not to reach large numbers, rather to have the teaching available for those who hunger and desire solid meat, and will be used to start a new movement of spiritual depth, strong commitment and doctrinal distinctness. Committed people tend to gravitate to our material.

Similar services followed in Sydney and Brisbane—capitals of New South Wales and Queensland respectively. At Parramatta, NSW, such numbers came to a meeting in the church hall of St John's, that the venue had to be changed to the cathedral itself. The response to the work of Grace to You—with its office in Sydney—was especially noteworthy. By August 21, John had spoken twenty-five times in eighteen days, interspersed with a few days of vacation. As they flew north to Singapore on that date, his final reflection on a first visit to the Antipodes was, 'Great need for biblical, powerful preachers and strong spiritual leaders.' Of course, he had seen little of a vast land but few discerning Australian Christians would have differed in their assessment.[1]

With the flight to Singapore they left the winter of the southern hemisphere behind them, and their winter clothes were sent home. Singapore, 'an island nation, seventy-five per cent Chinese, at the tip of the Malay peninsula', constituted an impressive introduction to the Far East: 'Bustling and beautiful, clean and uncluttered, amid tree-lined parkways, with the most

---

[1] In his journal, MacArthur agreed with the words of A. W. Pink: 'The great need of Australia today is for God-sent and God-anointed men, who will not shun to declare the whole counsel of God; men in whom the Word of Christ dwells richly; men on whom rests the fear of God, so that they are delivered from the fear of man.' Iain H. Murray, *The Life of Arthur W. Pink* (Edinburgh:Banner of Truth, 1981), p. 42. An enlarged edition of the Pink biography was published by the Trust in 2004.

efficient subway in the world', there was much to fascinate them. Among those to welcome them on arrival was twenty-eight year old Alex Lee, the enthusiastic local organizer of Grace to You tape and book ministry. That lives were being touched by that ministry was evident at a meeting of over a thousand mostly young people, of whom MacArthur noted:

> Great interest, eagerness to buy books, tapes, especially Lordship book—sold out! Spoke on Matthew, Gospel According to Jesus. Rich dialogue after. I was amazed to have such a response half way around the world—with people I didn't know—but who knew me.

Equally good discussion arose out of Question and Answer session at a visit to Singapore Bible College:

> Same questions as at home. The church is always needing clarification on the issues of qualifications and disqualifications for membership; women in leadership; sin and reformation; how to handle unbiblical elders; how to change the church tradition to conform to Scripture.

Experiences less familiar than those at home included a ten-course Chinese banquet, with a first taste of octopus, and a first visit to a crocodile farm. Among his overall impressions of the Christian scene were the 'strong evangelical association, good people in leadership, and much activity'.

On Thursday, August 25, the family left their pleasant rooms on the 24th floor of the Westin Plaza, unaware of quite how different their situation would be before the day was over. Singapore was not typical of the East.

A flight to Bangkok was uneventful, but there was a hint of future problems when they sought to transfer to their on-going flight for Delhi: 'They had erased our reservations off the computer and informed me we had no seats. After an hour-and-a-half hassling, we got on—scattered in smoking section; eventually we swapped seats to be together.' Their first night in India consisted of five hours sleep at the Imperial Hotel. The building was shared with rats and cockroaches; and, with no hot water, it had long since ceased to warrant its proud name. The next morning saw them out of doors, on a two hundred km bus ride to Agra and the Taj Mahal; but any respite was countered by the mental discomfort over much they had to witness:

> Incredible to see Delhi—a sea of destitute poor, teeming people, animals, and cars. I had the feeling I was seeing human society at its lowest social level. The poverty is consummate, everywhere—outside a beautiful government building, or a politician's estate, the poor live on the street with their shacks of straw, mud, cow dung, brick, plastic, or canvas, huddled in tiny places only their gaunt little bodies could fit.

When they arrived back at the Imperial at 10 pm that night it was with 'chaotic impressions of this strange and tragic land . . . Vast wasteland reeking with the feel of demonic presence.' There came home to John, as never before, a sense of the 'despair, deprivation, and pain' that must belong to hell itself.

A tour within Delhi arranged for the Saturday was only half taken. A meeting with Christian leaders at the YMCA that evening underscored the reason for their being in the country. Some fifty men gathered in a room so hot that the many fans almost drowned the human voice. Even so, there was good listening, and some evidence that the work of Grace to You India was reaching people. The extent of the need in evangelical churches, however, was stunning. Doctrinal interest was minimal: 'The need seems to them so desperate that they don't care what the theology is.' As a result neither the dangers of liberalism on one hand, or of 'easy-believism' on the other, were recognized. Nor was there any warning of ecumenism from evangelicals. 'I estimate', the visitor reflected,

> our tapes will either turn the tide of this softness or make me unpopular because those who accept the teaching will pose problems to the 'establishment'. At the end of his life, A. W. Tozer said he had preached himself off every Bible Conference platform in America—that may happen to me in India.

The next morning, Sunday, MacArthur preached at the Apostles' Methodist Church, and the message was summarized by the pastor in Hindi. In the evening he preached to 250 at the Delhi Bible Fellowship. In contrast with his brief presence, books could be permanent, and he believed that too strongly to leave their circulation to others: 'I am leaving *The Gospel According to Jesus* with all the leaders I meet.'

The first day of their second week in India, August 29, took them by air to Calcutta. On what followed their escape from the chaos of the airport, he wrote:

> Boarded a hot steamy bus for ride to Baptist Mission Society guest house right in the heart of the city. The streets were small, crowded, shacks, shantys, and broken sidewalks were home to thousands. Many rivers and ponds appeared along the road, filled with busy people, swimming, bathing, washing clothes, with water buffaloes, cows, and smells nothing short of sickening embedded in all of us.

Their accommodation proved to have few assets apart from its 125 years of history. A blackboard at the guest house designated their names and room assignments—for them a tiny room with two small beds, and for the five young people more of a barrack-type room with six beds. Conscious of the need to avoid gastro-intestinal infection, they had some apprehension on seeing their lunch prepared on the floor, but at least the floor was stone and not cow dung. The only sight-seeing they were to do was to take place that Monday afternoon. Two of the most frequently visited tourist spots were within walking distance from the Mission House, and, with misgivings, they scrambled along sidewalks, between dogs, people, and filthy oozing drains to these locations. Naked children, pleading for money, were on all sides:

> Patricia, with her tender heart for the little ones, found it especially difficult to give them nothing. They sensed her sympathy and so clung to her in clumps. We resisted giving them anything on account of urgent advice given to us on how to act in urban centres.

Their first stop was at Mother Teresa's convent where they spent some time with the aged lady whose care for the sick and dying had made her famous. They were impressed with her success in recruiting helpers, with the abundance of medical supplies, but sad at the vacuum where gospel truth was needed. Conversation with Mother Teresa revealed a very vague understanding of Christianity. 'All my people die beautiful deaths', she assured them. 'I love and respect all religions, but I love my Jesus.' But in a city where Hindus believe Jesus was the seventh incarnation of Shiva, and Krishna the eighth, the 'Jesus' was not presented as the only Lord, Saviour, and Mediator. Nor had

Roman Catholic teaching helped Mother Teresa in that regard. 'May you enter the heart of Jesus through Mary', she wrote in the Bible of one visitor.

If this convent visit was disturbing, still more so was their second stop that afternoon. 'Crushed between the dilapidated buildings of the crowded city, and down an obscure alley next to Mother Teresa's home', they found the temple of Kali, the wife of Shiva, a member of the Hindu trinity of gods (Brama, Vishnu, and Shiva). This appeared to be the religious focal point of Calcutta, and the place where animal sacrifice was carried on every afternoon at 3 pm. Amid noise and incense, demon worship was busily in progress, including the disgusting worship of a male phallus:

> Staring Satan's worship cold in the face was a chilling experience—my inside felt icy though I was dripping with the sweat of heat and sickness. To think that Mother Teresa was there and helping people physically but not confronting Satan's hellish domain was sad. It all looks so hopeless and so dishonouring to Christ. I felt I had really seen the kind of idolatry the Old Testament speaks of and there was a form of Christianity tolerating it. Truly these are a people in bondage to fear all their lives.

MacArthur's feelings in the temple of Kali were akin to those of the psalmist when he wrote, 'Indignation has taken hold of me, because of the wicked who forsake your law' (*Psa.* 119:53).

Despite the precautions they had sought to take at meals, by the first evening Matt was very sick, with severe cramps, rigours, vomiting, etc. John got through a meeting with some church leaders at the Baptist Church next door, only to succumb to the same symptoms later that night. The next day was their twenty-fifth wedding anniversary. With their rooms now like an infirmary it was to be unforgettable. Engagements at Serampore had to be cancelled, and John did not move from his bed except for necessities. Patricia had stomach pain but 'was a gracious nurse and tended to me'. Never in his life did he feel so uncomfortable; the heat was stifling and an open window only added to the oppression as crow-like birds in trees outside filled the air with loud and ugly noise.

> Sometimes I thought the sense of isolation from my life at home would never end. This went on all day and night—no one went anywhere except to get medicine. I am sure that when William Carey came to Calcutta it was a much nicer place—quieter, cleaner, and not devastated by fourteen million people.

The Tuesday night was only their second in Calcutta; it seemed they had been there a great deal longer. Of it he wrote:

> Another sleepless night filled with intermittent prayer that the family would be well and me for the busy schedule in the Philippines. I prayed for the church, the elders, people, many I knew had needs, for the students, for the radio/tape work, for my partners in ministry, feeling badly I couldn't give Patricia a better day.

When the morning came—Wednesday, August 31—they were able to get to the airport, 'quietly and somewhat bent over, longing for cool, clean air'. When, at last, they boarded a Thai flight for Bangkok, a cold orange juice 'tasted like it came from heaven'. A night in Bangkok aided the recovery of the invalids who were not yet able to take anything more than soup and drinks. John's journal note read: 'I threw my shoes away—they were covered with such filth and odour that they were not recoverable!' The next day, Thursday, September 1, took them across Cambodia, Vietnam, and the China Sea to Manila, where there was time to relax by the coast before first meetings on the Saturday.

Of all the places visited thus far, Christian work in Manila had known the most of John MacArthur's ministry. For some years his preaching had been heard over FEBC radio, and personal contacts with Grace Church had prompted the start of two Manila churches where he preached. He was struck by the unity among Christians of different denominations and the youth-fulness of so many of his hearers. Everywhere the people were 'open, warm, happy, and responsive'. The fact that the preacher shared the same family name with the Philippines' World War II liberator, Douglas MacArthur, added to the exuberance of the welcome he received. At an unplanned book-signing event, the crowd of 5,000 became so crushing that an assistant could only stop it by taking away his pen.

There was only time for five crowded days in the Philip-pines; it was enough to impress upon the family the character of numbers of the believers. 'The church', John observed, 'is made up of the common, humble people', and he saw the grace of God in them.

After Manila, one of the most eagerly anticipated visits of the whole tour still lay ahead as their plane descended to the spec-tacular airport of Hong Kong, 'with all the islands, blue ocean, mountains, and high buildings'. Before them was a first week in China. The first three days were spent in Hong Kong itself, largely in meetings with individuals, all concerned by differing means for the spread of the gospel across mainland China. One pastor, who had spent twenty years in prison, gave first-hand news of the house churches in Wuhan. Another leader, Jonathan Chao, was organizing literature work, and the two men did an interview which was broadcast. Chao's hope was to have Grace to You material translated into Mandarin for radio ministry into the mainland.

On the Friday they all crossed by the Boeing Jetfoil to the mainland, each carrying Bibles and study books. The first stop was Macau where, at the evangelical church of Pastor Lam, they were heartened by the serious, aggressive evangelism in progress. On a huge map of the city every neighbourhood was identified, with notes on the taking of the gospel to them. But the time MacArthur prized most in Macau was to stand at the grave of Robert Morrison (1782-1834), first Protestant missionary to China:

> Since no missionaries were allowed, he came as an employee of the East India Company. For over twenty years, in solitude (the graves of his wife and son, who died before him, are next to his), he hid alone in an upper room and worked on a Chinese language dictionary and the translation of the Scripture. It was a very moving experience to stand beside his grave. I felt very deeply the sacrifice, and meditated on his dedication. The millions of Chinese Christians in the underground church today reflect the fruit of his labour.

A river, and some four or five check points, separated Macau from 'Red' China.[2] The visitors went across and, with their

---

[2] At that time Hong Kong was still a colony of Britain, and Macau of Portugal.

books, passed guards without incident. After walking through a busy market, they proceeded to a cemetery where evangelicals were given a chapel building for use only on Sundays. Otherwise it was kept locked and unused. At this building they were shown a window, deliberately left broken, through which books could be put. Here they left MacArthur's *The Church the Body of Christ* and other books in Mandarin and Cantonese. Numbers of titles had previously been received by believers in that location by the same means; such 'dropping points' for books being a common means for the distribution of Christian literature.

Leaving the city behind, they were taken by their guide along side roads into the countryside, where they were all surprised by the beauty, 'the greenest hills and fields we had seen since New Zealand':

> We walked through obscure, out-of-the-way villages, visiting the homes—completely unexpected and unannounced—and always, no matter how poor, they offered us hot tea! Very gracious—as are the Asians in general. They laughed with us, as Esther interpreted, and showed us humble homes, asked us to sit down—to see the kitchen and their board beds with mosquito nets.
>
> We came to a town of 250,000 and met the pastor of that Three Self Church. He is a believer, but his church is totally controlled by the government. It is their way to show the world that they have religious freedom, but the pastors of these churches are old. The authorities want the church to appear to die a natural death when this old generation is gone. The house church movement on the other hand is illegal, but is vital and growing. Jonathan Chao estimates fifty million Christians.

They were back in Hong Kong for meetings on Saturday and Sunday. On the Saturday he spoke, through an interpreter, to about one hundred pastors on twenty marks of a ministry of integrity, followed by another valuable Question and Answer session. The final engagement was a service the next morning at Kowloon Baptist Church.

Only one leg of the tour now remained, and it began as they reached Seoul late in the evening of September 11. The airport was full of welcoming flowers and banners, intended, however, not for them but for athletes who were arriving from all over the world for the Olympics, which were about to be held. The MacArthurs' coming to Korea, however, was not unrelated to the Olympics. For the next three days John was to speak every morning (with simultaneous translation) to the five hundred to six hundred delegates of the World Congress of Sports. 'I love to talk to athletes', he noted, 'especially those serious about ministry for Christ.' After the second day, he wrote in his journal, 'It was important to be clear, simple, direct, and speak slowly. I tried.' They saw the Olympic stadium and village, where they met the USA basketball team and chaplains. Other hours in a full week were taken up with visits to orphanages, two pastors' conferences, an army base, churches and the Seoul Theological Seminary.

Somehow there was time to form an impression of Seoul— 'clean, modern, efficient, and a city of beauty'. But it was the believers he met who made the deepest impression on him:

> The Korean Christians are amazing—prayerful, daily quiet time, love to sing, joyful, not materialistic, and happy. God has really blessed them. They are humble and respectful. So many of the unsaved are in Asia that these Asians are the vital resource to be trained to reach their continent. We need to be on radio in Seoul.

At the same time there were some features that gave him concern. The world's so-called 'largest church' in Seoul left him entirely unimpressed: 'The services are wild and noisy—mixing Christianity with pagan worship; major emphasis on prosperity and healing.' Another common danger was more subtle and less often recognized. It was a near worship of education, giving a too high priority to degrees for the Christian ministry—'The pursuit of doctorates is a major issue—credentials are very important—much too important.' Coupled with this was the high status given to pastors, a factor that could prompt students, looking for the pastoral office, to start more new churches than was necessary. An eagerness for overseas degrees was also leaving too many Korean believers open to the influence of foreign academic institutions which held to Scripture in a much looser way than did the builders of the church in Korea. An example of this was to be seen in the guest house where the MacArthurs stayed (the Asian Center for Theological Study), and where a professor from Fuller Theological Seminary took a seminar on 'the integration of psychology and theology'.

As MacArthur and his family took the overnight flight home on September 16, there was still much to write in the conclusion of his journal. Two-and-a-half hours out from Los Angeles the final sentences read:

> Much to pray about as the dawn comes up through the windows of this 747. Didn't sleep on the eleven hours flight—too much thought about all we have experienced. I pray that all the experiences of this wonderful trip will enrich our lives and ministry and greatly impact the effect of our service to the Lord.

Two comments are needed to round off this chapter. How did MacArthur get time to prepare messages for so many engagements in the crowded weeks since the beginning of August? The answer is that he took with him about twelve sermons on themes fundamental to the needs of churches, which he had no hesitation in repeating. Most used of all was a sermon on the sufficiency and authority of Scripture from Psalm 19, on which a humorous note in Patricia's handwriting has survived. It seems to have been scribbled in a service at some point in the tour and, passed to another member of the family:

> Marcy says—if Dad gets sick anywhere along the way there are seven of us that could preach Psalm 19 for him! If you are not sick yet—you will be by the time church is over with all the hacking and sneezing and coughing over your shoulder. Get the SYRUP out!

But the preacher was not diverted from giving that subject first place, with other sermons on such themes as the right knowledge of God, and true versus temporary conversion. Deep impressions were made by these sermons in many places.

The journal shows that the preacher went on this tour as a learner as well as a teacher. In all the churches he found things to be admired—in 'tragic' India he noted, 'Many people sacrifice for the Lord here.' In the Philippines he saw how Americans could gain from the example of 'the humble servant hearts' of believers. In Korea he said of the Christians, 'We could learn so much from them.'

This first visit to the southern hemisphere and the Far East bore lasting fruit, an indication of the Lord's blessing upon it. Although most of these places would not be visited by MacArthur again, he would never forget the impression they had made on him. His sense of debt to others was deepened, and in the years ahead there would be unwavering commitment to an increasingly worldwide ministry. The room in the home of Vern Lummus, where the first recording was preserved in 1969, had led to the opening of a door to help millions.

9

Controversy

The Gospel According to Jesus was a MacArthur title published shortly before his tour across the Pacific in 1988. As will have been noticed, it was the book he gave to a number of pastors during those weeks away. In some ways this was to be the most important book of his life, bringing together issues that had become increasingly urgent to him through the years.

Eight years passed between John's first mentioning of this projected title to Phil Johnson at Moody Press and its final publication. It was not that it had been put on one side. In the Preface, John affirmed, 'This book has consumed my thoughts and much of my time for nearly four years.' It had also provided a subject for much discussion among his staff at Grace. Lance Quinn, who became Associate Pastor in 1986, recalled some of it when speaking with MacArthur many years later:

A small group of your close associates began to think with you about the implications of evangelicalism's weak gospel presentations, so many of these presentations being reinforced through books with equally weak theology, and which were so greatly disturbing to you (and to us) at the time. We began earnestly to discuss, reflect, research, and then ultimately see the release, in 1988 by Zondervan, of one of your most significant books, *The Gospel According to Jesus*.

That this book was published by Zondervan, and not by Moody (as Phil Johnson had promised MacArthur), requires comment. Moody had issued a contract for the title in 1982, as already mentioned, but while the book was still being written, a problem arose. Moody's leading author at the time was Charles C. Ryrie of Dallas Theological Seminary, and he was also one of the leading proponents of the position being refuted in *The Gospel According to Jesus*. When Moody learned that the book would quote from Ryrie and critique his teaching, they asked John if the book could be toned down so as to reflect no disagreement with Ryrie. When John assured them that this was impossible, rather than risk the danger the book threatened, Moody preferred to withdraw from their contract with the author.

There was another reason why *The Gospel According to Jesus* was seen as a doubtful venture. It had become customary among publishers to believe that titles majoring on doctrine would never find a large market or command attention. MacArthur recalls, 'Several publishers warned me that the book was "too doctrinal" to sell.' Yet a best-seller was exactly what *The Gospel According to Jesus* became. In the words of Phil Johnson, it was 'an instant worldwide blockbuster'.

In the Preface MacArthur wrote,

My prayer is that this book will provoke discussion, arouse prayer and self-examination, and lead ultimately to a resolution of these issues within conservative evangelicalism.

Given that his case questioned the presentation of the gospel supported by 'almost every Bible College or Seminary', he knew the controversy that Moody Press had feared was unavoidable and immediate. John H. Gerstner called the effect of its publication 'an ecclesiastical earthquake'. This was inevitable, for the case for gospel preaching, which MacArthur presented, challenged a great deal of contemporary teaching. His Preface paid tribute to many with whom he disagreed—'many are my friends'—but insisted on the serious nature of the difference:

> Other controversies have generated more heat and spawned more print, such as questions on prophecy, modes of baptism, styles of worship, and so on, but these are truly peripheral to the real issue. The gospel is not. It *is* the issue.

MacArthur's case was that current teaching had

> subtly changed the thrust of the gospel. Instead of exhorting sinners to repent, evangelicalism in our society asks the unsaved to 'accept Christ'. That makes sinners sovereign and puts Christ at their disposal . . . This modified gospel depicts conversion as a 'decision for Christ' rather than a life-transforming change of heart involving genuine faith, repentance, surrender, and rebirth unto newness of life.[1]

Against this, MacArthur argued that *more* than faith is involved in a true conversion. Saving faith is never without a new birth, making the individual 'a new creation' and indwelt by the Spirit of God who has brought this about. To explain how 'converts' continued to lead worldly lives, the popular teaching held that a person could be a Christian without personal holiness; he might accept Jesus as Saviour but not yet 'as Lord'.

---

[1] *The Gospel According to the Apostles,* p. 74.

For MacArthur, this was alien to the Scripture: 'Any "salvation" that does not alter a lifestyle of sin and transform the heart of the sinner is not a genuine salvation.'[2]

His critics dubbed this teaching as 'lordship salvation', claiming that it was error to treat moral change as necessary to conversion for that would be to introduce 'works', whereas the sinner's justification is by faith in Christ *alone*. Typical of that view were the words of one critic, quoted by MacArthur:

> 'Of course Jesus taught a lordship message', one old-line dispensationalist brother wrote me. 'He was preaching to a people under law. Under grace we must be careful to preach a grace message.'[3]

In the extensive controversy on this subject the issue was often confused. As MacArthur observed, an age used to sound-bites and little theology was poorly placed to understand what was at the heart of this issue. Some, who were ignoring that conversion entails more than a changed legal standing before God in justification, thought he was jeopardising the truth of justification by faith alone. They failed to teach that grace secures a decisive break with sin, demonstrated by repentance and new obedience. 'True saving faith is a *repentant* faith in Jesus Christ, and that produces good works.'

What is more, when an individual is savingly convicted of sin, he or she desires more than forgiveness; such a person wants salvation from sinfulness; he is ready to pray, 'Save me from myself!'

> Salvation is for people who hate their sin. It is for individuals who understand that they have lived in rebellion against

---

[2] *The Gospel According to Jesus,* p. 79.
[3] *The Gospel According to the Apostles,* p. 35.

a holy God. It is for those who want to turn around, to live for God's glory.

To bring individuals to that awareness, preachers should follow Christ's example in dealing with the rich young ruler: 'Evangelism must take the sinner and measure him against the perfect law of God so that he can see his deficiency.'[4] 'Don't be afraid to teach your children what God's law demands . . . The law's moral standards give us the necessary foundation for understanding what sin is.'[5]

Conversion has a human side and a divine side. On the human side the promises of the gospel supply the warrant for immediate repentance and trust in Christ; yet this will not happen where there is no conviction of sin. It was at this point that Dispensationalism missed the significance of the law of God in the Ten Commandments. It supposed that 'law' means self-effort, and salvation by works. But such was never the purpose of the law. The law, in its revelation of the character of God, and of man's obligation to love Him 'with all your heart, and with all your soul, and with all your strength, and with all your mind' (*Luke* 10:27), brings home the seriousness of human sin. The law demands repentance, but

> when Christ demanded repentance, he was not calling sinners to self-reform. In fact, authentic repentance

---

[4] Ibid., p. 84.

[5] *Successful Christian Parenting*, p. 55. One reason many evangelicals are afraid of teaching the Ten Commandments is their concern lest the fourth commandment should be regarded as obligatory. In the Question and Answer session at the 1997 Shepherds' Conference, MacArthur indicated that was no good reason to be silent on the law. He believes that while the ceremonial aspects of the law, instituted at Sinai, are no longer for Christians, it is right that 'Sunday is set aside for celebrating the finished work of the Saviour', and good that believers attend public worship both morning and evening.

begins with the sinner's recognition that one is hopelessly in bondage to sin and powerless to change. Jesus' classic example of repentance was a tax gatherer who came to understand his hopeless position . . . This publican's conversion demonstrates how repentance is far more than a simple adjustment of one's opinions about Christ . . . While there is no question that repentance involves a change of mind, it certainly does not end there. It is a wholesale change in direction, a change in purpose, a change in attitude, and a change of affections. All of this can only be the result of God's gracious regenerating work and is therefore evidence of true salvation.[6]

Modern evangelism had gone wrong in confusing the relationship between the human and the divine in conversion. Man is responsible to repent and believe; both are essential parts of evangelistic preaching; yet both are gifts of grace and will not be found until there is a change in human nature at its deepest level. The saving sight of Christ (which is faith) depends on 'God's initiative and power . . . Spiritual sight is a gift from God that makes one willing and able to believe . . . The result of spiritual sight is a surrendered, worshipping heart.'[7]

MacArthur was charged with displacing 'grace' by introducing the moral element into conversion. On the contrary, he replied, it was the teaching he was opposing that reduces the place of grace. It makes the human 'decision' the controlling event, and leaves salvation in the sinner's own hands. But the grace that saves is greater than his critics were recognizing:

---

[6] Address on 'The Glory of True Repentance', in *Assured by God*, ed. Burk Parsons (Phillipsburgh, NJ: P&R, 2006), pp. 131-2.

[7] Ibid., pp. 73-5. No doubt it was on account of such statements that MacArthur was accused of being a hyper-Calvinist. His book, *The Love of God* (Dallas: Word, 1996), shows how mistaken that charge is. He says, with Calvin, 'the Father loves the human race' (p. 85).

True grace is more than just a giant freebie, opening the door to heaven in the sweet by and by, but leaving us to wallow in sin in the bitter here and now. Grace is God presently at work in our lives. By grace 'we are His workmanship, created in Christ Jesus for good works, which God prepared beforehand, that we should walk in them' (*Eph.* 2:10) . . . That ongoing work of grace in the Christian's life is as much a certainty as justification, glorification, or any other aspect of God's redeeming work.[8]

MacArthur had been brought to see the issue which Warfield had referred to in his review of Chafer quoted earlier—the truth rediscovered at the Protestant Reformation, that 'knows no determining power in the religious life but the grace of God', had become mixed with error 'from the laboratory of John Wesley'. Rather more accurately in the American scene, MacArthur traced the error that Chafer, and much of Fundamentalism accepted, to Charles G. Finney, who taught that man does not have a fallen *nature:*

He concluded that people are sinners by choice, not by nature. He believed the purpose of evangelism should therefore be to convince people to choose differently—or as many would say today, 'make a decision for Christ'.[9]

'He taught that salvation required no sovereign regeneration by God, but only the act of the human will.' This led, as MacArthur goes on to say, to the whole apparatus of 'altar calls' and to the 'easy-believism' which it inevitably promoted.[10]

---

[8] *The Gospel According to the Apostles,* pp. 32-3.
[9] *Ashamed of the Gospel,* p. 158. See also the extended Appendix, 'Charles Finney and American Evangelical Pragmatism', pp. 227-35. The pervasiveness of this teaching in Fundamentalism is scarcely open to question. George W. Dollar wrote that 'Most Fundamentalists . . . would have refused to adopt any statement of the Five Points [of Calvinism].' *History of Fundamentalism,* p. 276.
[10] *Hard to Believe,* pp. 83-4.

MacArthur's follow-up title to *The Gospel According to Jesus* was *The Gospel According to the Apostles,* from which I have already quoted. Written five years after the first book, it added substantially to the biblical argument. In his Preface MacArthur regretted that

the overwhelming majority of criticisms have nothing whatever to do with biblical matters. Some reviewers have complained that the lordship issue is too divisive, the message too hard, or my position too dogmatic. Others have argued semantics or taken exception to my terminology. Some have feigned indignation, claiming *The Gospel According to Jesus* is an unfair personal attack on them, their friends, or their organization.

Zane Hodges, Professor of New Testament at Dallas and a leading critic, believed that MacArthur had fallen into 'the error of the Puritans'. Hodges charged the Puritans with corrupting the Reformers' doctrine of justification by faith, and called the Puritan teaching on faith and assurance 'a tragic blemish on the history of the Christian church'.[11] While MacArthur's position was in no way dependent on the Puritans, it is true that his reading of church history had confirmed his convictions. He wrote:

---

[11] Zane Hodges, *Absolutely Free!* (Grand Rapids: Zondervan, 1989), p. 32. This same accusation was introduced to British evangelicals by R. T. Kendall, who takes the same Antinomian position as Hodges, and is quoted by MacArthur as writing: 'The person who is saved—who confesses that Jesus is Lord and believes in his heart that God raised Him from the dead—*will go to heaven when he dies no matter what work (or lack of work) may accompany such faith.* In other words, no matter what sin (or absence of Christian obedience) may accompany such faith.' *Once Saved, Always Saved* (Chicago: Moody, 1983), pp. 52-3 (italics in original). Kendall argues that Paul's warning in Ephesians 5:3-6 does not concern exclusion from heaven. Further on this, see my *David Martyn Lloyd-Jones: The Fight of Faith* (Edinburgh: Banner of Truth, 1990), pp. 721-6.

The preponderance of Bible-believing Christians over the centuries have held these to be basic tenets of orthodoxy. They are the standard precepts of doctrine affirmed, for example, by all the great Reformed and Calvinist creeds.[12]

He documents that assertion in an appendix to *The Gospel According to the Apostles,* and also answers the argument, loved by some critics of the Puritans, that they represented a departure from Calvin. A quotation from Calvin epitomises exactly where MacArthur (and the Puritans) stand. The Reformer wrote:

> We must take care not to separate what the Lord perpetually conjoins. What then? Let men be taught that it is impossible they can be regarded as righteous by the merit of Christ, without being renewed by His Spirit unto a holy life . . . God receives none into His favour who are not also made righteous.[13]

The lordship controversy had not died down before another was to follow. It related to a subject MacArthur had first faced while preaching through 1 Corinthians in 1976. California was in many ways the starting point for the Charismatic movement; and, by the mid-seventies, its main ideas had gained wide acceptance and popularity across the nation. Disturbed by this development, in his preaching on that Epistle MacArthur included a series on the Charismatic Movement; published in 1978 as *The Charismatics: A Doctrinal Perspective.*

---

[12] *The Gospel According to the Apostles,* p. 25.
[13] Ibid., p. 161.

While his treatment of the subject anchored his own church, it had a limited hearing in the wider evangelical scene as the movement continued to spread and gain acceptance. By 1979, it is said, nineteen per cent of all Americans identified themselves as charismatic or Pentecostal.[14]

In 1992 MacArthur published a revised and fuller treatment of his earlier book under the title *Charismatic Chaos*. In the Preface he wrote, 'I sincerely thank God for the many charismatics who sincerely love the Lord and want to obey Him.' But he did not regard that sentiment as justification for saying nothing on the issues. For a time he seemed to be largely alone in his conviction that the new teaching was threatening evangelicalism through a back door. His case was that the enthusiasm for revelatory prophecies, and for apostles today, ignored the uniqueness and sufficiency of Scripture. To the argument that the movement was divinely authenticated by the renewal of miraculous gifts, he replied that Scripture, and not alleged experiences, is the test. He pointed out how many contemporary 'prophecies' had been proved false by the test provided in Scripture (*Deut.* 18:21-22). Yet this was brushed aside by the promoters of the Charismatic movement. Feeling and phenomena were being made the focus of attention, not Scripture and doctrine. While its central message—'the baptism of the Spirit'—claimed Scripture for its support, charismatic belief was guilty of reconstructing biblical teaching on conversion when it argued that 'salvation does not really give us everything we need for spiritual victory. We are still lacking; we need something more.'

[14] Richard Quebedeaux, *The New Charismatics* (San Francisco: Harper & Row, 1983), p. 84.

In challenging this thinking, MacArthur is careful to show that the issue is *not* for or against more experience of God. It is about how that experience is to be gained:

> Lifeless, dry orthodoxy is the inevitable result of isolating objective truth from vibrant experience. But the answer to dead orthodoxy is not to build a theology on experience. Genuine experience must grow out of sound doctrine. We are not to base what we believe on what we have experienced. The reverse is true. Our experiences will grow out of what we believe.
>
> The Holy Spirit is working mightily in the church today, but not in the way most charismatics think. The Holy Spirit's role is to empower us as we preach, teach, write, talk, witness, think, serve, and live. He does lead us into God's truth and direct us into God's will for our lives. But He does it through God's Word, never apart from it . . . to use phrases such as 'God spoke to me', or 'This was not my idea; the Lord gave it me', or 'These aren't my words, but the message I received from the Lord', confuses the issue of the Spirit's direction in believers' lives today.[15]

MacArthur's case is that, instead of leading to true revival, the Charismatic movement takes Christians in the wrong direction:

> No genuine revival or orthodox movement has ever been led by people whose authority is based in any way on private revelations from God . . . A longing for something new and esoteric has replaced historic Christianity's settled confidence in the Word of God—and that is an invitation to Satan's counterfeit.[16]

Some who in 1992 thought the word 'counterfeit' too strong, revised their judgment after the so-called 'Toronto Blessing' at

---

[15] *Charismatic Chaos* (Grand Rapids: Zondervan, 1992), p. 65.
[16] Ibid., pp. 58, 73.

the Airport Vineyard Church in that city in 1994. Once again the advocates of this phenomenon claimed that the 'extraordinary events' were proof that the work was of God. In what was meant to be a favourable report, an article in *Charisma* declared: 'On a typical evening, dozens of people can be found lying or rolling on the floor or laughing uncontrollably.' William De Arteaga sought to silence any criticism of these happenings with his book, *Quenching the Spirit*. Together with other Toronto supporters, he appealed to the awakening in the time of Jonathan Edwards to justify what was happening at the Airport Vineyard. But MacArthur was able to show that an authentic appeal to Edwards proves the very opposite, for no one was stronger in refusing to allow the mystical and the emotional to displace the test of Scripture.

The controversies considered in this chapter warrant observations.

North-American Indians, when travelling by river, were said to be able to detect the approach of dangerous rapids well before they came into sight. It is the business of Christian leaders to see dangers before others see them. This has been a very necessary feature of MacArthur's ministry at a time when the toleration of errors has almost become regarded as a virtue.

He saw that the main issue in the Lordship controversy was vitally related to the health of the churches.

The teaching that sought no recognition of Christ's lordship in conversion had grown out of thinking which gave no place to the law of God. But instead of law being contrary to grace, it is, Paul affirmed, by the gospel that 'we establish the law' (*Rom.* 3:31). Christ died 'that the righteousness of the law might be fulfilled in us' (*Rom.* 8:4). In other words, salvation's purpose is to restore man to the likeness of the God whose image is revealed in the holiness of the law. Certainly it is true that 'free from the law' means deliverance from its condemnation through Christ. The law cannot be the basis of justification for believers, for Christ has fulfilled its demands and penalties in their place. But the moral perfection which the law displays remains a rule for their lives. Exemption from the law, in that sense, would be no blessing at all.

MacArthur grasped this truth when few others were speaking to it: 'Those in Christ are no longer under the ultimate penalty of the law, but are far from free of its requirement of righteousness.'[17]

He saw how it was this wrong teaching on conversion, combined with the setting aside of the law, that had brought on superficial Christian living and worldliness in the churches. 'A gospel of grace cannot be preached to someone who has not heard that God requires obedience and punishes disobedience.' For lack of this teaching, a casual light-heartedness, with little attention to the seriousness of sin, had become commonplace among evangelicals. Such conditions were not new to church history, but the old term for the phenomenon had long been forgotten. MacArthur revived the right word: 'No-lordship theology is classic Antinomianism [*anti-nomos* = anti-law]. There is no way around that fact.'[18]

---

[17] *New Testament Commentary, Matthew 1-7*, p. 272. See also pp. 253-9.
[18] *The Gospel According to the Apostles*, p. 96.

The problem is that most people do not think of God as someone to be feared. They don't realize that He hates the proud and punishes evildoers. They presume on His grace. They fear what people think more than they care what God thinks.[19]

MacArthur was no less going against a popular trend when he spoke against the teaching behind the Charismatic movement. Most evangelicals took the view that, whatever the differences, this was no subject for controversy. And many thought it would take time to judge whether the movement was beneficial or otherwise.

MacArthur, on the contrary, believed that the teaching of Scripture was enough to give a sound judgment on the subject. He also knew that the distinctives of charismatic belief were not new to the twentieth century. They have appeared at a number of times in the course of church history, always bringing short-term excitement and ultimate confusion. Charismatic thinking was advancing because contemporary evangelicalism was indifferent to the history of the church:

Old certainties are often met with automatic suspicion just because they have been affirmed by generation after generation of evangelicals. These days it is fashionable to question everything.[20]

The nub of MacArthur's warning was that charismatic thinking was teaching people to look to the extraordinary and the sensational instead of to the Word of God. By the contemporary claim of supposed revelatory gifts, the finality of God speaking

[19] MacArthur, *The Vanishing Conscience* (Nashville: Nelson, 1995), p. 100.
[20] *The Truth War*, p. 144.

in Scripture was being undermined. In many circles 'experience' was being placed above truth, emotion above thought, and the consequence was little careful regard for the teaching of the New Testament. In addition to *Charismatic Chaos,* several of MacArthur's most important titles major on this danger.[21]

What these controversies confirmed to MacArthur was that the beliefs many evangelicals accepted or avoided were determined too largely by influences other than Scripture. To be passionate about truth was ceasing to be a mark of Christian character. A. W. Tozer had noted this ethos before his death in 1963:

> The fashion now is to tolerate anything lest we get the reputation of being intolerant. The tender-minded saints cannot bear to see Agag slain, so they choose rather to sacrifice the health of the Church for years to come by sparing error and evil; and this they do in the name of Christian love.[22]

MacArthur was grieved at the number of preachers who adopted a 'code of silence' when 'contentious issues' were raised. Their comment was, 'We are committed to keeping peace among brethren and unity in the body of Christ.' 'I was astonished', he wrote, 'to realize how many Christians think the Charismatic movement lacks biblical support, but are reluctant to say so aloud.'

---

[21] Particularly the titles, *Reckless Faith* and *The Truth War.*
[22] J. L. Snyder, *In Pursuit of God: The Life of A. W. Tozer* (Camp Hill, PA: Christian Publications, 1991), p. 128.

Take an uncompromising stance on almost any doctrinal or biblical issue, and a chorus of voices will call you obstinate, unkind, heartless, contentious, or unloving, no matter how irenically you frame your argument.[23]

At the same time, if there has to be controversy, he insists it be without 'abusive, spiteful, or venomous behaviour towards others'.[24] 'Controversy frankly is distasteful to me. Those who know me personally will affirm that I do not enjoy any kind of dispute.'[25] There is also, he warns, the permanent need for humility:

We do indeed need to exercise caution in making judgments about the gravity of someone else's error. We must never judge superficially. We need to remember that we are indeed prone to misjudgments and errors of our own. 'We all stumble in many things' (*James* 3:2).

But whether or not to 'contend earnestly for the faith' is simply not an option. A faithful pastor has to warn and guide. He has to be negative as well as positive. He cannot leave the field to others. Some have disparaged MacArthur's writings as 'books for untrained laymen', as though Christians at the pew level are not of first importance. His comment on that kind of observation is relevant:

Doctrine is not the exclusive domain of seminary professors. All true Christians must be concerned with understanding sound doctrine . . . Doctrine forms the belief system that controls and compels behaviour.[26]

'It is exceedingly difficult in these times', wrote Spurgeon, 'to

---

[23] *Reckless Faith,* p. 46.
[24] *Reckless Faith,* p. 107.
[25] *Ashamed of the Gospel,* p. xx.
[26] *The Gospel According to the Apostles,* p. 22.

preserve one's fidelity towards God and one's fraternity among men. Should not the former be preferred to the latter if both cannot be maintained? We think so.'[27] To which quotation John MacArthur adds another from the same preacher:

> What have you and I to do with maintaining our influence and position at the expense of truth? It is never right to do a little wrong to obtain the greatest possible good . . . Your duty is to do the right: consequences are with God.[28]

---

[27] C. H. Spurgeon, *The Sword and the Trowel* (London: Passmore & Alabaster, 1887), p. 196.

[28] Grace to You letter, February 1995.

8. Patricia MacArthur.

10

Patricia MacArthur

*T*he family is the one environment where your devotion, faithfulness, and consistency matter most. It's where the most is at stake. It's where the greatest blessings can be realized. There is simply no greater earthly blessing than raising your children in a way that honours God, and then seeing them grow up to honour God with their own lives.[1]

Such words carry the greater conviction spoken in a congregation where all know that the pastor and his family enjoy the blessing of which he speaks.

John MacArthur has said much on Christian family life, and the church at Sun Valley has seen what he speaks about. By the time the above words were in print his own four children were grown-up and he could write, 'It is a delight to see them beginning to raise their little ones in the nurture and admonition of the Lord.'

Godly homes are blessed, and under God the first persons responsible for that blessing are Christian wives and mothers.

[1] John MacArthur, *Successful Christian Parenting*, p. 201.

'Men have the authority in the home, but the women have the influence. The mother, more than the father, is the one who moulds and shapes those little lives from day one.' This should not be understood as though fathers need have minimal spiritual input. When the children were growing up, John was always present for family prayer and on this point he has written:

> From the very beginning of our marriage more than twenty-nine years ago, Patricia and I committed ourselves not only to creating healthy individual habits for deepening our walk with Christ, but also to cultivating them in the life of our family. For us and our four children, the breakfast table was the spiritual rallying point in our home. We began each day gathered around the table, sharing breakfast and reading from God's Word. Children are keen at picking up on patterns, so it didn't take ours long to realize how seriously we took the things of the Lord.[2]

For Patricia her children had the first place in the pattern of her life. As she would say in later years, 'I never sacrificed my kids for anything or anyone. The time when they are young can never be recaptured.' But devotion to children does not mean the absence of discipline, and many things were not left to their decisions when they were young: there were chores for them to do; Sundays were for church and spiritual things; friendships were under parental control; on such things as theatre-going, junky magazines, 'sleep-overs', television in their bedrooms, Patricia says, 'the kids had no option'. She saw it as her responsibility that the children should learn convictions on behaviour from infancy.

---

[2] Grace to You letter, September, 1993.

The MacArthur children had the blessing of long-living grandparents. Grandfather Dale Smith lived to his ninety-ninth year, dying in 2009. John spoke of him 'as a tremendous example'.

Patricia's mother, Lorraine Smith, remained a support to all the family until her death in May 2001. Irene MacArthur died suddenly while visiting one of her daughters in Arizona in February 1999.[3] Grandfather Jack MacArthur was called home on June 15, 2005, at the age of ninety-one. Only in January of that year did he conclude teaching Sunday School at First Baptist Church in Eugene, where he had formerly been the pastor. John was with him during the last month of his life, and at a Memorial Service would speak of him as

the first model of a minister I ever saw . . . above reproach in his life and ministry to the day he died, though aware of his sinfulness and need of God's grace. Dad drummed into me the importance of standing for the Lord in conviction, conduct, and character.

While both John and Patricia see the mother's role as of first importance, it is not, for them, the key to a happy Christian home. That lies further back, they insist, in the marriage relationship itself:

The love between husband and wife is the real key to a thriving family. The properly situated family has marriage at the centre; families shouldn't revolve around the children. Furthermore, all parents need to heed this

[3] John said of her: 'The degree to which I have enjoyed success as a father, as a husband, and as a minister of the gospel, is a result of the investments she made in me each day.'

lesson: what you communicate to your children through your marital relationship will stay with them the rest of their lives. By watching how mother and father treat one another, they will learn the most fundamental lessons of life—love, self-sacrifice, integrity, virtue, sympathy, compassion, understanding, and forgiveness.[4]

Even so, that is not the foundation. 'Marriage for two Christians is first of all commitment to Jesus Christ and then to each other.'[5] Only then will priorities be in the right order: for the woman, 'love for heaven, husband, and home'.

In a home where this is true, the original purpose of creation is being fulfilled.

Eve was created to be a helper to Adam—to keep him company, to support and encourage him, to work alongside him. Her role as his wife was a token of the marvellous grace of God to man.

She was in no way an inferior character made merely to serve him, but she was his spiritual counterpart, his intellectual co-equal, and in every sense his perfect mate and companion.[6]

For John MacArthur, his wife is as truly the gift of God as was the first gift to Adam. Without Patricia his whole life and ministry could not be what they are. He leans on her, as she leans on him. On their fortieth wedding anniversary in 2003 he would write: 'Through Patricia, God has filled our home with love, grace, and kindness. He has provided for me a godly partner and a daily source of joy, support, and accountability.'

[4] John MacArthur, *Twelve Extraordinary Women* (Nashville: Nelson, 2005), p. 95.
[5] Ibid., p. 233.
[6] Ibid., p. 5.

If whom we marry is the next most important thing to conversion itself, it is doubly so for every pastor. John Watson, advising students for the ministry on this point, warned that of all men they 'ought to be most careful in the choice of a wife, for she may be either a help or hindrance not merely to his comfort but to his work'. A good wife, he continued,

> advises her husband on every important matter, and often restrains him from hasty speech . . . receives him weary, discouraged, irritable, and sends him out again strong, hopeful, sweet-tempered. The woman is in the shadow and the man stands in the open, and it is not until the woman dies and the man is left alone that the people or he himself knows what she has been.[7]

MacArthur would have no doubt about the truthfulness of Watson's words. He would go further and say with Spurgeon,

> A true wife is the husband's better half, his flower of beauty, and his heart's treasure. In her company he finds his earthly heaven; she is the light of his home, the comfort of his soul.[8]

In an interview reported in the Talbot students' magazine, the *Tiger Tale* (February 1980), Patricia MacArthur is described as 'a friendly, open, and energetic person'. At that date her share in the work of the church included chairing a weekly deaconess meeting, and in taking care of the wives of seminary students.

[7] John Watson, *The Cure of Souls, Yale Lectures on Practical Theology 1896* (London: Hodder and Stoughton, 1896), pp. 235-6.
[8] *Spurgeon's Practical Wisdom, or Plain Advice for Plain People [John Ploughman's Talk & Pictures]* (Edinburgh: Banner of Truth, 2009), p. 95.

But she saw her first calling as the provision of a secure and peaceful home for her family.[9] To successive years of young people, preparing for Christian service, her priorities would be passed on by word and example. In the *Tiger Tale* interview already quoted, she said:

> It's a big job to raise four children and keep the house according to my standards. We have all heard stories about 'pastors' kids'. Rebellious kids can invalidate a man's ministry. I want our children to be honouring to John's ministry.

Beth Quinn, wife of one seminary student in the 1980s, was to thank Patricia MacArthur for many things. They included: her friendship, 'allowing access to you and John so freely'; 'being transparent, always answering my questions in an honest and biblical way'; 'praying for our family through the joys and trials of family and ministry issues'; and 'for just being you'.[10] The seminary students themselves learned from Patricia. In the words of one of them, Tom Pennington,

> You modelled for us that wives can be our greatest confidants, our most helpful critics, and our wisest counsellors. By your own consistent tenderness toward those in special need, you taught us that pure religion and undefiled is to care for those who are most vulnerable and needy.[11]

Patricia did not hide the fact that, as a young pastor's wife, she had not learned everything at once. For example, she did

[9] Patricia MacArthur fully shares these convictions of her husband: 'One generation plants the trees and another gets the shade. Our generation lives in the shade of many trees that were planted by our ancestors.' 'Mothers are the makers of men and the architects of the next generation.'

[10] In a letter to Mrs MacArthur, read by her husband, Lance Quinn, at a dinner in which former pastoral staff celebrated John MacArthur's fortieth anniversary, 30 Jan. 2009.

[11] Part of speech at the fortieth anniversary dinner.

not instantly accept that the first call on her husband's time was not always her own.

> I used to complain about not having John's attention and company whenever I wanted it, but I realized he deals in eternal matters. He needs to be free to follow up opportunities offered by the Holy Spirit.

It is not John MacArthur's habit to refer in sermons to his wife and family, nor ought it to be for any pastor. But we know enough about his home to know that the principles he taught on family life were lived out. For instance, on the biblical teaching respecting a wife's submission to her husband, he is careful to say what it does not mean. It does not mean a wife losing her own personality, or giving up her own opinions.

> There is nothing to prohibit a man from seeking his wife's counsel about such matters as where the family should live, what job offer he should accept, whether the family should participate in this or that activity, or a host of other similar decisions. In fact, the man who is not interested in his wife's opinion in such matters is a foolish and uncaring husband. But the final decisions are ultimately the husband's prerogative, because he is the one who will be accountable to God for the stewardship of his family.[12]

In the home Patricia exercises her own influence on John's life and ministry. She can propose changes as no one else can. 'I still need to remind him sometimes to take time for the family', she said in 1980. Making sure there were enough occasions for relaxation was one of her roles. Family evenings were times 'to sit around and talk or play games together'. When the boys had sports days at school, John was an enthusiastic onlooker

---

[12] *Successful Christian Parenting*, p. 188.

without any prompting, and in due time they would join him in his own favourite exercise of golf.

A faithful wife will have opportunities to remind her husband of humility, as Patricia did on one unexpected occasion. At six o'clock one morning in their home, they were shaken awake. While earthquakes are not uncommon in southern California, at the 6.8 level on the Richter Scale this was no normal tremor. As John later described it:

> The doors started banging, the kids were flying out of bed, and the radio newscaster reported that the dam above our house had broken and everybody had to evacuate. By God's providence, the only thing we lost was a shelf full of my athletic trophies. We went into the den and they were in a pile on the floor, the symbols of my long-ago gridiron glory, smashed to bits.

As they looked at the scene, 'My wife used the opportunity to remind me that God blesses those who are humble.'[13] It was no light-hearted remark. To undergird this council, years before she had inscribed for him in needlework the words, 'Walk humbly with thy God.' This gift he mounted at eye level in front of his desk in his study.

Occasionally when close friends are visiting the MacArthurs they are amused to hear Patricia say, 'Now Johnny, you know that's not right', and to hear him acquiesce. He certainly values her judgment, and happily leaves most of the financial affairs of the home in her hands. One feature of her character on which he depends is her awareness of the needs of individuals in the congregation. In her own childhood home Patricia had been familiar with the high place that belongs to service to others.

[13] *Hard to Believe,* p. 107.

Two of her sisters had gone to the mission field. When she was no longer responsible for leading the meeting of deaconesses at Grace Church, it made no difference to her practice. 'Her strength is people', MacArthur says.

> She will come into my study and put down a piece of paper on which there is a list of people who are ill, or who have special needs, or should have a 'thank you', or some kind of a response from me. And she will say, 'I want you to write or call these people.' She feels in a way I do not, and if I can keep involved in people's lives it is largely because of Patricia.

In describing their normal daily timetable, as it was in 1980, Patricia said: 'I lead a very sheltered life. Johnny takes the kids to school in the morning and returns at 5.00 in the afternoon.' Some ten years later this routine had a major change when her husband decided to move his study from church to home (now some twenty minutes from the church in a country location). It had become increasingly difficult for him at the church to get the privacy he needed for preparation and study. Inevitably the removal of his books entailed some difficulty but, once happily resettled, there came a problem in the new arrangement that had not been anticipated. In his words:

> Patricia said it's so wonderful to have you at home, I can make you lunch and bring you tea. Of course, with phones ringing and kids around, I needed to keep the study door shut. From time to time she would come up to the study and in her usual happy way make an observation or ask, 'Honey, can I ask you a question?' Then there would be a pause as I disengaged myself before I might say, 'What do you want?' Or she might come with some lovely food prepared and hear only some kind of grunt from me. After a

few days of these experiences, she commented: 'You know, I think it might be better for our marriage if you go back to the church.' She was not angry but hurt at the new situation in which I was present and yet not available.

All settled down as John recognized his responses were not appropriate!

In late July 1992, they experienced a trial that would test the faith they believed and taught to others.

One afternoon John was at a golf course anticipating some of the others to join him. He was waiting for their eldest son Matt, coming in one car, with his mother driving behind with Melinda. They were driving on a winding, four-lane road when, to his horror, Matt saw his mother's car catch soft earth beside the inside lane, then flip in the air and turn over. The seriousness of the accident was instantly clear, and a helicopter was called to take mother and daughter for emergency care. John was phoned, and he would later speak of that call as the moment when his 'whole life suddenly changed'. There were no details, only that Patricia was gravely injured and was being airlifted to a hospital about an hour away from where he was:

> Inadvertently leaving my golf clubs on the practice tee, I immediately got in my car and headed for the hospital. That hour-long drive to the hospital will be forever etched in my memory. A thousand thoughts flooded my mind. I realized, of course, that I might never see Patricia alive again. I thought of the gaping hole that would exist in my life without her. I reflected on the essential part she has had in my life and ministry over the years. I wondered how I

could ever manage without her. I remembered when we first met, how we grew to love each other, and hundreds of other little things about our life together. I would give anything to keep her, but I realized now that choice was not mine to make.

The questions that entered my mind were, How am I going to live my life? How am I going to step into all her roles? I kept thinking, What will the children do? I cannot meet their needs, the needs that only she can meet. What will the grandchildren do? What will our life as a family be without her? (for Patricia really is the glue that holds everything in our family together). It was just one huge mystery, and I was very much aware of the fact that there is no one whom I had ever met who could replace her. There is no one who could step into her shoes to fulfil what she does. Yet I didn't have a time when I did not believe that God was in charge. That thought never entered my mind, but this one did: What if she was gone, what in the world were we all going to do, and how would we put our lives back together?

A supernatural peace flooded my soul. My grief, sorrow, uncertainty, and fears were all enveloped in that restful peace. I knew that Patricia and I were both in our Lord's hands, and under the circumstances that was the only place I could imagine any sense of safety.

When I arrived at the emergency room, I learned that Melinda had been badly bruised and cut but was not seriously injured. She was severely shaken but not in any danger.

A doctor came out to explain Patricia's injuries to me. Her neck was broken. Two vertebrae were severely crushed. The damage had occurred above the crucial nerves in the spinal cord that control breathing. In most cases like hers, the victim dies immediately.

Months of special care followed, with Patricia's head held immobile in a steel frame, held by four rods fixed to a plastic upper-body vest. John had now the treasured experience of being able to serve the one who had ministered to him for so long. Slowly Patricia was out of danger, but her extremities remained numb. Prayer was widespread, and there was slow recovery until only her right arm continued to suffer paralysis. One day she asked John to ask specifically 'that the Lord will give me back my right arm'. 'Lord, we want your will to be done', he prayed, 'but I'd like to ask you if your will couldn't be full restoration.' In time the prayer was answered.

Eighteen months after the accident Patricia recorded her own testimony in speaking with Richard Mayhue:

> The accident affirmed that our days are numbered and God is in charge. That is what I kept emphasizing to our daughter who was in the accident with me—1. that God is in control of our lives and, 2. that He is totally sovereign. Whatever He allows to come into our lives, He has a purpose for our good and His glory. And, 3. it made me realize how temporary this life on earth is.
>
> People ask me, 'Why do you think God allowed this to happen?' or, 'What did you learn through it?' I've learned again that God is sovereign; He will go through any circumstances with us. The verse that kept going through my mind is, 'Thou wilt keep him in perfect peace, whose mind is stayed on Thee' (*Isa.* 26:3). I used to sing that a lot in the morning. I know His salvation, and I have come to know His healing powers in a personal way.[14]

---

[14] Richard Mayhue, *The Healing Promise* (Fearn, Ross-shire: Christian Focus/Mentor, 2001), p. 249. This book contains a whole helpful chapter on Patricia MacArthur's accident and its lessons.

At the same time, Patricia MacArthur was careful to note that an answer to prayer for healing is not in any way related to our deserving. Two especially valued friends who visited her when she was still in hospital were Joni Eareckson Tada and her husband Ken. Joni, in her wheelchair, and with the experience of twenty-five years of paralysis, said, 'Oh, Pat, I'm so glad you are not a quad', and sang to her, 'His Eye is on the Sparrow'.

Mindful of such Christians as Joni, Pat has said:

> Certainly our prayer is not necessarily answered according to our spiritual state. I think it is what the Lord sees best for everybody involved. In my situation, there were many people aware of and praying for my healing and recovery because of the effect it would have on John's ministry. The Lord saw fit to answer the prayers according to the way they were asked—not because I was deserving of this particular kind of healing. There is no question that God orchestrated these things to bring glory to Himself. I'm just thankful that He chose me to be a recipient of His undeserved and unexplained grace.

In reflecting on what had happened in these months MacArthur was to conclude:

> This whole experience has been the most difficult trauma in our lives together. Yet through it all Patricia and I have learned again—in a very practical way—that faith works. Our faith in Christ—the same faith with which we first trusted in Him as Lord—has remained strong and enabled us to trust Him through this trial.[15]

In her interview in 1980, Patricia MacArthur advised that 'life-partners need one heart and one mind to have a successful

[15] *The Gospel According to the Apostles,* pp. 18-19.

ministry'. That union in Christ was all the stronger for the suffering of 1992. It was strong confirmation to her in her role, as she said afterwards, 'The Lord has given me a heart for service, which I enjoy and love.' And it cannot be doubted that the added grace given to her reflected to others in her husband's continuing ministry. In a book dedicated to her in 2008, he wrote:

> To my beloved Patricia, who personifies faithfulness. Her love and devotion to me have been my greatest earthly delight since the earliest days of my ministry. When she has had to relinquish me because of my pastoral duties, or settle for a distracted husband because of endless writing projects and sermon preparation, she has borne those trials with exemplary grace and patience. For every grief I ever caused her, she has given me a thousand blessings in return—not the least of which is a wonderful home and family that are held together and adorned by her loving attention.[16]

---

[16] *The Gospel According to Jesus, Revised and Expanded Anniversary Edition* (Grand Rapids: Zondervan, 2008).

11

A Correction and an Example from Russia

*T*he 1980s had seen large growth in the ministry on all fronts. The possibilities seemed endless. But I turn now to a development which was not to prove successful and from which valuable lessons were to be relearned.

In November 1987 'The Master's Fellowship' was established at Grace. Under this title the main agencies for outreach were brought together under a governing board to which new supporters belonged, and fresh initiatives were launched with additional hired staff. One purpose was to plan MacArthur's speaking ministry around the country, instead of leaving it too largely dependent on the invitations of others. Another aim was to expand the influence presently exercised among pastors by the Shepherds' Conferences. After the first such conference in 1980, a further ten were held by 1985, and attendance continued to grow. Accordingly a 'Master Conference Schedule' was published detailing the date and place arranged for more than forty 'Shepherds' Seminars' across the United States in the period April 1988 – November 1989. This was announced in the pages of the Grace to You letter, and in the same issue readers were informed that a Christian audio magazine called *Forefront* was now available.[1]

The most conspicuous development from the Master's Fellowship, however, came with the launch of *Masterpiece* in the summer of 1988. This was a full-scale magazine/journal, produced in a gloss and colour format, and in style the equal to any of the world's leading periodicals. In the first issue MacArthur, as Senior Editor, explained that the formation of The Master's Fellowship was not his idea, but it had come out of a belief that

> we are on the threshold of even greater things. I have seen Him bless His truth not only through a dynamic local church, but also in a worldwide media outreach, a flourishing college and seminary, a unique missions ministry, and extensive service to church leaders . . . The Fellowship has four clearly defined areas of emphasis: Communications, Education, World Outreach, and Church Resources.

MacArthur connected the title of the new magazine with Ephesians 2:10, 'We are His workmanship, created in Christ Jesus for good works'—'to create in us a masterful work of grace'. Three issues of *Masterpiece* were published in 1988 and a further fourteen were to follow. The material was well-balanced and, while serious in tone, pitched at a popular level: it included a 'Cutting Edge' editorial from John, teaching from leading authors (old and new), short Christian biographies, help on family and parenting issues, Questions and Answers, and book reviews. In its doctrinal orientation the pages promoted the rediscovery of an older evangelicalism, and the books reviewed

---

[1] Grace to You, Spring 1988, 'Introducing a New Ministry'.

majored on such authors as James I. Packer, A. W. Tozer, and
Martyn Lloyd-Jones. In one issue MacArthur was asked to list
the books that had the greatest impact on his life. He named
the following:

> Arthur Bennett, ed. *The Valley of Vision: A Collection of
> Puritan Prayers and Devotions* (Banner of Truth, 1975).
> Stephen Charnock, *The Existence and Attributes of God*
> (Klock & Klock, 1977).[2]
> J. I. Packer, *Knowing God* (Inter-Varsity, 1973).
> D. Martyn Lloyd-Jones, *Preachers and Preaching* (Zonder-
> van, 1971).
> D. Martyn Lloyd-Jones, *Studies in the Sermon on the Mount*
> (Eerdmans, 1977).
> Arthur Pink, *Spiritual Growth* (Baker, 1971).
> John R. W. Stott, *The Preacher's Portrait* (Tyndale,
> 1967).
> Thomas Watson, *The Beatitudes* (Banner of Truth,
> 1975).
> Thomas Watson, *A Body of Divinity* (Banner of Truth,
> 1970).

In *Masterpiece* there was a combination of good content, style,
and promotion. A major success would have been a reasonable
anticipation, and yet, after seventeen issues, it stopped without
notice in the summer of 1992. It had failed.

The sudden termination must have been a surprise to most.
A discerning reader of its issues may have judged from the
frequent changes in the names of the editors that there were
problems, and there was some irregularity in publication dates.
Phil Johnson was 'editor' in the first issue, but thereafter his

---

[2] These volumes have been reprinted by the Banner of Truth as vols 1 &
2 in the five-vol. set *The Works of Stephen Charnock* (2010). See MacArthur's
comment on Charnock's greatest work, p. 203.

input was only occasional. His main attention was elsewhere, in the preparation of MacArthur books for publication. Tom Pennington and Mike Taylor gave their best efforts to the magazine, but a few new men on the scene, including Robert D. Van Kampen, General Director of the Board of The Master's Fellowship, were not entirely of the same mind on its content. The setting up of the Fellowship as an umbrella organization had been Van Kampen's idea, and he saw it as a promotional agency. A wealthy man himself, he may have thought that spending money liberally would generate wider influence. When this did not happen, and debt began to exceed revenue, there were stronger appeals for monetary help than had ever been made before. MacArthur chafed at this situation, and in the summer of 1990 told Phil Johnson to 'get back into it'. At the same time Van Kampen dropped out. 'These were volatile years', Johnson would later comment. Certainly the enterprise had not been marked by the harmony present in earlier years. By the time a halt was called a debt had built up that would take an estimated five years to clear.[3]

When MacArthur became certain they were on the wrong track, he terminated the Master's Fellowship—in Johnson's opinion, 'the best thing he ever did'. In a letter of March 19, 1992, addressed to all friends of Grace to You, MacArthur began:

> I'm writing to ask your forgiveness. I also want to explain some changes you will be seeing in the mail you receive from Grace to You.
>
> The Lord has led us to carefully re-evaluate this important aspect of our ministry. With great sadness I realize my

[3] In fact, the debt was cleared within two years.

letters to you each month have begun to be monopolised by appeals for money. On behalf of all our staff, and from my heart, I want to ask your forgiveness for that. I confess I had become careless and was beginning to let the ministry wander from the principles I have always espoused.

Seven years ago, a listener wrote to ask my fund-raising philosophy. At that time I replied:

'We don't say much about money either on the radio or in print, because I am a little resistant to the idea of appealing for funds. I see too many ministries today trying to raise money in ways that just don't honour the Lord . . .'

We were slipping off track for a while, but I want you to know I still hold those convictions with all my heart. I have often said that my concern is the depth of my ministry: God will take care of the breadth of it. Or, as the Apostle Paul indicated, we simply plant seed and water it—God causes growth (*1 Cor.* 3:6). Clever fund-raising techniques, money, and human effort can never impel a ministry like ours to grow faster or larger than God Himself graciously permits. Moreover, the Lord will always provide support for any ministry that honours and serves Him.

I know that the Lord called me to minister, not to raise funds. So I am reviewing my commitment to the real priorities: teaching the Word and meeting people's spiritual needs.

The reader of these words would suppose that the fault had been in the writer, and, as the leader, MacArthur believed that it was. He had allowed developments which were against his better judgment. In another letter to friends of Grace to You, March 15, 1993, he wrote:

You may recall that one year ago this month, after much prayer, we made deep cuts in our ministry budget, enacted several changes in the mail we send to our ministry family, and re-committed ourselves to depending on God's provision for our financial needs. As anyone knows, during times of change you'll always weather a few anxious moments, we've weathered a few of our own.

The last sentence was an understatement. It was just four months after his 'apology' letter of March 19, 1992, that Patricia's serious car accident occurred. These were trials that carried abiding instruction, and to this he referred in several letters:

Patricia's near-fatal automobile accident and the events that have unfolded since then have certainly brought many humbling lessons. My life—each of our lives really—is indeed a vapour, and only through God's grace do any of our plans ever materialize.[4]

During the past year God in His sovereignty has brought into my life some extraordinary events—events that have in a wonderful way united my personal circumstances with powerful truths from God's Word . . . God taught us many lessons during those difficult days . . . We don't exist for the sake of raising money or building a huge ministry empire. We exist solely to teach the Bible, and we trust God to sustain us at the level He chooses.[5]

As I mentioned in a letter a few months ago, we made several deep cuts in our ministry budget last year, including several painful decisions that affected our staff size and the extent of our outreach. I can tell you that God is clearly blessing our commitment to trimming our financial obligations and living within our means . . . We still have many challenges ahead, and don't want to presume on God's blessing.[6]

[4] Grace to You letter, October 16, 1992.
[5] Ibid, June 17, 1993.
[6] Ibid, August 16, 1993. In this letter MacArthur expressed the hope that

While the above was happening, spiritual lessons were being confirmed to MacArthur from an unexpected quarter. When the Berlin Wall fell in 1989 the Communist world of Eastern Europe and the Soviet Union was suddenly open for the gospel. He made an initial two-day visit to Leningrad (St Petersburg) in July 1990, his party taking three hundred Bibles with them, donated by the senior class of the Master's College. These were readily distributed, including to five border guards, and one to a taxi driver who turned out to be a Christian. Presented with a Bible in Russian the taxi driver pressed it to his heart with joy and gratitude.

An invitation to Baptist churches in Russia soon followed the initial visit. John hesitated. His short visit had impressed him with the greatness of the need, and there was no doubt about the welcome he had received when he preached at a three-hour-long service during the July visit. But he was uncertain whether taking advantage of the opportunities in the former Soviet bloc was consistent with his calling to his local church. In addition, he was not enthusiastic about speaking to congregations through an interpreter—'The language barrier can make teaching tedious for both speaker and audience.'

However, he accepted the invitation and returned to Russia. He was not only to find people helped by the Word of God but to have his own life and thinking enriched.

Masterpiece might be resumed sometime in the future. This was not to be.

Between October 22 and November 2, 1990, he preached at pastors' conferences in Moscow and Kiev, and spoke at the Odessa Bible School. Some 20,000 copies of his book, *A Master Plan for Church Leadership* had been translated into Russian, funded by the congregation at Grace, and 1,500 copies were eagerly taken up within a few days.

In the October of the next year he spoke at Bucharest for the Union of Baptists pastors in Romania. Three-and-a-half days of meetings had been planned, and around 200 pastors were expected. Instead 500 came to hear MacArthur speak on 'Expository Preaching' and 'Church Leadership'. The schedule of meetings from 9.00 in the morning until 8.30 at night was evidently flexible, for on one day the visitor found himself on his feet teaching and answering questions for eight hours at a stretch. From there he went on by train to another pastors' conference at Kiev, in Ukraine (October 7-12, 1991). About eight hundred men were present and, again, the length of the meetings was unpredictable. A morning Question and Answer time planned for one hour went on for three.

The experience of these two years, 1990-91, made a deep impression on MacArthur. The spiritual hunger was unmistakeable, and yet half the churches in Ukraine were without pastors, and some two hundred towns and villages around Kiev were without any evangelical church. His enquiry for their greatest need got the response, 'We need pastors—pray that God will raise up young men to be pastors.' 'If I could speak Russian', he was to say on his return home in 1991, 'I'd be there and stay until God moved me because that is the great harvest field.'

The contrast between material conditions in the former Soviet bloc and the affluence of the West could not be missed.

In Leningrad, for instance, he learned of four families living in a four-room apartment, with thirty-one people dependent on the same bathroom. Yet the life of the churches seemed in no way weakened by the general deprivation; on the contrary, there was remarkable vitality and strength. A difference in the pattern of church life could not be missed. While much regarded as indispensable for success in America was absent, such was the hunger for the Word of God that there was no problem in maintaining crowded services morning and evening on a Sunday, as well as services on Tuesday, Thursday, and Saturday nights. Reflecting on what he saw, MacArthur wrote:

> Their worship services were the very picture of austere simplicity—just the preaching of the Word and the celebration of the ordinances, totally devoid of the flash and entertainment being touted as essential tools for the times by all the 'experts' back home. That got me thinking more deeply than ever about how the Lord builds His church and what it means to be a wise master builder (*1 Cor.* 3:10-15).
>
> Slavic worship is simple and gospel-centred, exactly like we see in the book of Acts. The gimmickry, superficiality, and man-centredness that have spoiled so many western churches were notably absent.
>
> The stress is on the essentials: repentance from sin, faith in Christ, biblical preaching, obedience to the Word of God, love for one another, and a passion for the truth against all forms of error . . . I sat in many Russian worship services for hours, hearing convert after convert publicly repent—renouncing former sins and declaring faith in Christ to the gathered church. It was the polar opposite of what American church gurus insisted was absolutely necessary.

More than ten years later MacArthur would still underline these lessons to American audiences:

> Over the years I have ministered quite a lot in Russia, Ukraine, Belarus, and other parts of the former Soviet Union. The church in those countries, repressed by Communism for so many decades, is nonetheless vibrant and dynamic today. One of the significant things that struck me when I first began to minister there was the terminology that virtually all Russian-speaking believers use to describe conversion. They do not speak of accepting Christ as one's personal Saviour. They would never say merely that someone 'made a decision for Christ' or that the person 'invited Jesus into his or her life'. The language they use is simple and entirely biblical: the new believer is someone who has repented. If a person shows no evidence of repentance, he or she would not be embraced as a Christian, no matter what sort of verbal profession of faith was made . . . By contrast, we live in a culture of such shallow religion that most of what goes by the name 'Christian' in Western society has little or no emphasis on repentance of any kind. The call to repentance has been deliberately omitted from the most popular gospel presentations of our generation.[7]

From the beginnings of the 1990s MacArthur was to have a life-long bond with churches in Eastern Europe and beyond, and he contributes significantly to their witness. But the help he gained from them in strengthening his convictions was perhaps no less significant. Certainly, as his Grace to You letters of the 1990s show, he was emphasizing lessons not commonly heard in contemporary evangelicalism.

---

[7] Address on 'The Glory of True Repentance' in *Assured by God*, ed. Buck Parsons (Phillipsburgh, NJ: P&R, 2006), pp. 126-7.

One of these lessons had to do with the source of the greatest danger to the gospel. It does not come from the world's hostility to the church:

Your church's greatest enemy isn't the government, the culture, Hollywood producers, or the liberal media. Scripture states and history confirms that churches are strengthened under persecution and adversity. If our churches are to be destroyed, or rendered ineffective and stagnant, that will happen at the hands of her own people . . . One of my greatest fears for the church I pastor is that we would unwittingly abandon the vital principles that keep us healthy, growing, and strong. The day we cease clinging to those principles is the day we grow cold and dishonour God before a watching world.[8]

Another lesson was the falseness of the message which represented the gospel as a way to get more from God on the material level:

As I have studied God's Word and experienced both the exhilaration of spiritual victory and the discouragement of failure, I'm convinced the key to powerful living is not in getting more from God. The key is just the opposite. The moment we stop making demands on Him and offer ourselves as a living sacrifice is the moment we begin to please Him . . . From my own experience I know that being a living sacrifice is not an easy path. But sacrifice is absolutely necessary if we are ever to know the fullness of God's blessing and render to Him the service He is due.

[8] Grace to You letter, August 15, 1994.

9. A Shepherds' Seminar with John MacArthur in Russia, 1990.

10. John enjoying the Pacific, early 1960s.

11. The Chapel, built on Roscoe Boulevard in 1956, was the first structure on Grace Community Church's large campus. This painting of the refurbished Chapel was commissioned to mark the church's fiftieth anniversary in 2006. Church member, Dick Foslien, was the artist.

12. Ground-breaking for Grace to You at its new 2.79-acre site, January 21, 2000.

13. The new Grace to You building, opened April 24, 2001.

14. John and colleagues with students of the Master's College.

15. Dr MacArthur greeting a student, Master's Seminary in the background.

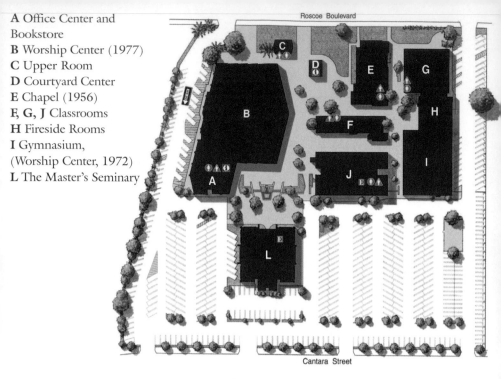

A Office Center and
Bookstore
B Worship Center (1977)
C Upper Room
D Courtyard Center
E Chapel (1956)
F, G, J Classrooms
H Fireside Rooms
I Gymnasium,
(Worship Center, 1972)
L The Master's Seminary

16. Grace Community Church Campus Map, 2010.

17. Architect's drawing of Grace Comminity Church Campus, which was used on a
Grace Community Church bulletin, 1977.

Grace Community Church of the Valley

"...holding forth the Word of life..." Phil. 2:16

13248 Roscoe Blvd. Sun Valley, Calif. 91352
John MacArthur — Pastor   782-5920

18. Some of the weekly volunteer helpers at Grace to You.

19. *Left to right:* Don Green, Phil Johnson, and Mike Taylor, celebrating the 25th Anniversary of Phil and Mike working for Grace to You, March 19, 2008.

20. Four generations: Jack MacArthur, with John, and eldest
son Matthew, and his eldest son, Johnny.

21. Almost the whole family, February 1, 2009,
courtesy of Lukas VanDyke.

As shown in photo (from left to right):

Back row: Olivia Gwinn, Kathryn Gwinn, Ty MacArthur, Johnny MacArthur,
John MacArthur, Kylee MacArthur, Andrew MacArthur, Brooke MacArthur

Middle row: Gracie Gwinn, Susannah Gwinn, Jessy MacArthur, Patricia
MacArthur

Front row: Tommy Gwinn, Mark Gwinn, Marcy Gwinn, Kelly MacArthur,
Matt MacArthur, Elizabeth MacArthur, Mark MacArthur, Erika MacArthur,
Melinda Welch, Oliver Welch, Kory Welch, Audrey Welch

By family:

Matt & Kelly MacArthur: Johnny, Ty, Jessy
Mark & Marcy Gwinn: Kathryn, Olivia, Susannah, Gracie, Tommy
Mark & Erika MacArthur: Kylee, Andrew, Brooke, Elizabeth
Kory & Melinda Welch: Audrey, Oliver, Eloise (b. 2010)

22. Dr MacArthur in the pulpit at Grace.

23. Patricia with John, 2009.

12

Grace to You

*I*f there was any delay to the work of Word of Grace (tape ministry) and Grace to You (radio and publishing) in the 'volatile years' at the beginning of the 1990s, it was only temporary, and both agencies were to surge forward in the following decade. Until 1985, the two ministries had operated from separate locations, the tape ministry from premises in North Hollywood, and Grace to You in a smaller building a quarter of a mile away. The two agencies naturally supported and complemented one other, so union was inevitable. In 1985, the two ministries formally merged and came together in a rented facility just one block from runway's end near the Burbank airport. A special soundproof recording studio was built to deal with the problem of air traffic, but within a few years, the ministry had outgrown this facility and another move was necessary.

In 1990 Grace to You moved to a more suitable rented facility in a business park in the suburb of Santa Clarita. The building, designed to house five small businesses, had just the right ratio of warehouse space to office space, and doors were cut between the sections to accommodate easier movement from one bay of offices to the next. It was not a very efficient layout, but the ministry fitted the building perfectly.

The building was hard hit by an earthquake that shook the entire Los Angeles area early on Tuesday morning, January 17, 1994. Although the epicentre was some fourteen miles away over a small range of mountains, the jolt was nowhere felt more strongly than in Santa Clarita. Just a few miles away from Grace to You several large freeway bridges crumbled and fell, and a building four blocks away collapsed entirely.[1] Amazingly, the Grace to You building withstood serious structural damage but all was chaos within, furniture and equipment having been thrown in all directions. When John visited that same morning, his first response at the sight of the damage was one of gratitude. 'Had the tremor come during working hours with a full team of staff and volunteers, we could have easily suffered severe injuries and even fatalities.'

It was not until the year 2000 that Grace to You finally obtained property and built a more suitable facility, designed specifically to meet the ministry's needs, in the Valencia district. Phil Johnson was Executive Director; he was joined by Don Green as Managing Director in 2004.

By 1998 there was the capacity to produce six hundred cassette tapes an hour, and eleven million had been sent out. Simultaneously sermons, and occasional programs, were provided for more than eight hundred radio stations. That same year the headquarters' staff of Grace to You consisted of fifty-two full-time men and women and 113 volunteer helpers from the Grace Church.

During the 1990s the ministry associated with MacArthur's books had seen new dimensions. A flow of major titles—drawn

[1] This was the Northridge Earthquake, already mentioned in chapter 10.

from his preaching—had come on to the market: *Our Sufficiency in Christ* (1991); *The Master's Plan* (1991); *Charismatic Chaos* (1992); *Ashamed of the Gospel* (1993); *Reckless Faith* (1994); *The Vanishing Conscience* (1994); *The Glory of Heaven* (1996); *The Love of God* (1996). These books were published by the regular publishing houses, particularly Moody, Nelson, and Crossway, but with Grace to You co-operating in a significant way. When *Our Sufficiency in Christ* was published in 1991, Grace to You took a large quantity from the publishers and gave free copies to all on the mailing list of MacArthur's monthly letter. Recalling this as a 'key turning-point', MacArthur wrote in 2009,

> We believed that even a small fee would limit the reach of that book for some people. Instead of selling a relatively small number, we gave away thousands of free copies and trusted God's people to support what we were doing as they were led and able. The response and growth we saw was amazing.

This same pattern was continued in the following years, both with books and tapes sent to those who got the newsletter. The free book was not necessarily one of MacArthur's. In 1994 it was the Banner of Truth title, *The Valley of Vision: A Collection of Puritan Prayers and Devotions*.

There was at first hesitation over whether this procedure should be followed when the major work, *The MacArthur Study Bible*, came out in 1997. It was a title considerably more expensive than any thus far offered, and free distribution seemed to represent a substantial risk. The decision was that any 'risk' was worth it. MacArthur remembers:

> We hoped for the best, prepared for the worst, and sent out more than 35,000 *Study Bibles*. The response was historic

. . . Gifts poured in as God's people shouldered the financial weight of our ministry in unprecedented ways.

In the opinion of Lance Quinn, the *Study Bible* has had 'greater impact around the world than all your other volumes'. Perhaps it is too early to make that assessment. We lack the perspective of time, but I am inclined to think that the most enduring influence of MacArthur's books may prove to be through the *MacArthur New Testament Commentaries* of which I will write in later pages.

By 1999 Grace to You had distributed 3,154,927 copies of MacArthur's books and study guides. Evidence came back that the occasional offer of free books was helping numbers of people with limited means. A cynical critic might think it was just a means of pressure selling, but evidence from the track record of Grace to You shows this was not the case. Free items go out without any strings attached, as can be seen in the current distribution of MacArthur sermons, which can be downloaded by anyone free of charge from the website. From 1969 to June 13, 2002, 13 million cassette tapes were produced, a number being sold at a moderate price. Since June 2008 the same sermons have all been available as MP3s on the internet, without cost. In the period from 2008 to January 2010, 14.4 million were downloaded in this way, to the great pleasure of all at Grace to You.

As had happened in America, the tape ministry also led the way for radio broadcasts overseas. In 1983 a South African named Peter Gruner attended the Shepherds' Conference at Sun Valley. He went home with a large number of sermon cassettes which he proceeded, on his own initiative, to duplicate and circulate in his own country. This led to Grace to You going to air with sermons on the SABC Network in South Africa. When John and Patricia made a first visit to South Africa in 1992, John was astonished at the number of radio listeners that he met. He wrote home:

> The beauty and majesty of God's creation here—although more breathtaking than I could have ever imagined—pales when compared to the transforming work God is orchestrating in people's lives. The response I've witnessed to our radio ministry here is unbelievable.
>
> I am told that in South Africa, more people listen to Grace to You than any other radio broadcast—that includes both religious and secular programs. Imagine what would happen to the United States—to our cities, our families, and our government—if the most popular radio program in our country was thirty minutes of Bible teaching!

One of the hearers he met was a thirty-five-year-old man by the name of Tienie. He had served as an army chaplain during the war in Angola, and was a minister in the Dutch Reformed Church, the respected pastor of a large congregation. But then, while listening to a Grace to You broadcast he was brought to the discovery that he was not a Christian at all. 'I cannot describe the joy I felt in meeting this man', said MacArthur, 'knowing that God had used something as simple as a radio to reach into his life and save him.'

MacArthur's preaching visits to South Africa in 1992, and again in 1994, were long to be remembered. Martin Holdt, veteran pastor in Johannesburg, is not alone in speaking of the 'special impact' of that preaching in the land. Joel James, another church leader, has written:

Because of the radio program, one church leader in South Africa has called John MacArthur 'a pastor to the whole nation'. That is clearly an exaggeration of monumental proportions; nonetheless, it gives a sense of the impact John's sermons, books, commentaries, and training ministry have had on Christians and pastors in this country. In the future, God willing, the impact of John MacArthur's ministry will continue to filter north to other gospel-needy countries. Like a pebble dropped into a duck pond, the ripples of John's ministry are spreading across the continent of Africa. Praise God for choice servants of Christ whom God uses in such special ways!

The first South African visit impressed on MacArthur the crucial work that can be done through broadcasting across the world. In 2009 he could speak of 'our daily broadcasts' as 'the most identifiable aspect of our ministry, bringing our verse-by-verse teaching to an audience of millions around the world'. The estimate of numbers was no exaggeration. At that date he was being heard on 732 outlets in the United States, and fifty-three outlets in nine other countries. In all these he was being broadcast in English, but in the year 2000 a Spanish-speaking pastor, Henry Tolopilo, joined Grace to You, and a Spanish department began. Starting with a broadcast on 'The Sufficiency of Scripture' in January 2000, Tolopilo took on the translating and preaching of MacArthur's sermons in Spanish under the title Gracia a Vosotros. These messages were soon to be heard through 716 outlets in twenty-five countries, including the USA where there is a large Spanish-speaking population. With the addition of the Spanish broadcasts, it was true to say that in 2009 John MacArthur could be listened to 1,979 times daily on 1,502 outlets in thirty-four countries.

Figures of this kind of magnitude begin to lose meaning, but while I was preparing these pages a letter from a friend in Ecuador made them more significant. Florence Judd is a missionary nurse in the town of Shell, and has some contact with the Shuar tribal area of Tsentsak Entsa, two days distant by foot, canoe, and bus, in the province of Morona Santiago. On a recent visit to these people, where there are no believers as yet, she was surprised to find Domingo, the headman, sitting alone in the radio room listening to John MacArthur in Spanish. 'I wouldn't have known it', Florence writes, 'except that I happened to pass by just as the theme tune for Gracia a Vosotros was being played and I recognized it.' She added that 'There are many listeners to the program in the Shell area, Christians listen more to radio here than they read books—broadcasts are more readily available and books expensive.'

The ministry of Grace to You, as MacArthur often recalls, began in 1969 in a shoe box, which kept the names and addresses of those who could not attend the Sunday services at Grace Church on account of illness. In a letter of May 2006 he marvelled at the way, through that ministry,

> every day of the year we have the opportunity, on a global scale, to shape the way people think about and study Scripture. The fact that our radio program, CDs, tapes, books, and website put us within reach of virtually everyone on the planet is staggering. We have a strategic opportunity to teach and equip men and women to study it for themselves.

This period saw many more preaching visits overseas. In 1995 MacArthur was to be in Brazil, Italy, and Russia; in 1996 Ireland, Scotland, and New Zealand; in 1997 England, Russia, France, and Switzerland (Geneva); in 1999 Ukraine, Germany, and Geneva; in 2000 Italy and Scotland. The many visits to Canada I will not attempt to list.

Before the turn of the century new technologies were bringing developments no one had anticipated. 'Already this year,' he could write in October 1998,

> I've had the joy of speaking at pastors' conferences in India, Russia, Switzerland, and Romania, all without ever leaving Southern California. Using video streaming technology, I'm able to teach, encourage, and fellowship with church leaders virtually anywhere in the world.

This was taken further in 2001 by the first use of video-teleconferencing, by which he could be both seen and heard live at a Shepherds' Conference in Berlin. The same means in 2002 brought contact with Victor Ryaguzov and his Transfiguration Church, in Samara, Russia. The use of this technology was to be repeated with pastors in a number of places in the years which followed.[2] Even Question and Answer sessions could be conducted by this method.

The technology did not mean the end of foreign visits, but it was well they could begin to be curtailed. The preacher passed the age of sixty in 1999, and the previous year there had been a reminder that his strong health might not be permanent. In August 1998 he had routine knee surgery but this was followed by life-threatening complications. Blood clots from his knee

---

[2] New Zealand (2002), Samara (2003), Berlin (2004-5, 2007), Zurich (2008), Romania (2008), Pune, India (2008), Italy (2009).

passed into his lungs, causing a pulmonary embolism. Prayer was followed by great thankfulness for his full recovery.

What MacArthur's visits to foreign countries meant to Christians is well stated by Solano Portela, Presbyterian leader and translator, who heard him at a FIEL Conference in Brazil:[3]

> I was impressed with his knowledge of the Bible. His message was coherent, clear, and proceeded from his heart. Above all, he would recite different biblical passages, quoting them from memory, during his message. I was very glad that I was not translating him, for certainly I would need to refer to my Bible constantly during the interpretation.
>
> MacArthur has had a tremendous impact on my life, and family, not only through his books and sermons, but in the overall influence of his ministry. We ended up sending three of our children to study at the Master's College, and have been blessed with the instruction they received ever since. His vision goes beyond the gates of the church, setting up an institution of Higher Education and a Seminary. In worldwide TV newscasts and talk shows, we have seen his steadfast witness to the Christian faith, speaking biblical truths on all kinds of issues that challenge our values and principles.

The opening in Italy came through another of those unplanned contacts. On a visit with a party from his church to

---

[3] Editora FIEL is an evangelical publishing house, founded by Richard Denham, which has contributed largely to a recovery of the doctrines of grace in Portuguese-speaking countries. An annual conference is held near Sao Paulo and in Portugal.

Israel in 1995, MacArthur formed a friendship with two of the party, Joe Aleppo, and his wife Georgia. Mrs Aleppo was the niece of Anthony Rossi, founder of the Tropicana Orange Juice Company. After leaving Italy in the 1960s, Rossi had become a Christian and among the Christian causes to which he devoted his subsequent wealth was the Aurora Foundation, a mission founded by him to support missionaries and church-planters in Italy. On the death of Rossi in 1994, Joe and Georgia Aleppo had inherited the responsibility for this mission, and their friendship with MacArthur came exactly at the time when they needed the aid of his leadership. It led to John making a first visit to Italy in 2000.

Evangelical work in Italy had long been small and fragmented. One hindrance to growth was an opinion prevailing among believers that any strong doctrinal preaching would only further weaken their unity. Joe Aleppo did not share that opinion, and he urged MacArthur to come and 'preach the doctrines of grace'. A first visit in 2000, and the first Focus Conference, confirmed Aleppo's conviction. For several men a new vision for preaching was born and long-term consequences were to follow. By 2007 MacArthur had led five of these conferences.[4] On the last visit, when Patricia was with him, they had the happiness of placing an Italian copy of the *MacArthur Study Bible* in the hand of an elderly believer by the name of Christiana. Her testimony was of special encouragement to them:

> Christiana is in her eighties, and for much of her life, she
> lived and worked in a Catholic convent as a nun. In fact,

---

[4] Other developments in Italy included the start of a radio broadcast of his sermons in Perugia, the English language being useful to numbers who come to that city to study languages.

she was Mother Superior, responsible for the spiritual leadership of the nuns in her convent. Christiana was only recently baptized and was excited to tell me how, so late in life and in such great darkness, she came to saving faith in Christ. She explained, through an interpreter, that for many years she and some of the other nuns in her convent had faithfully listened to Bible teaching on radio. It turns out they were listening to a Bible teacher I know, an Italian-born evangelist here in the United States who broadcasts his verse-by-verse teaching across Italy.

In an amazing demonstration of divine grace and patience, the truth triumphed over error and the light of God's Word dawned in the heart and mind of an eighty-year-old woman. Her bondage ended and her burden was released. I can't help but wonder what kind of ministry Christiana now has in her small corner of the world.

If his first visits to Russia confirmed to MacArthur what was needed in the United States, it is probable that his familiarity with religious conditions in Italy strengthened the convictions that had led him into a controversy at home which began in the mid-1990s.

In March 1994 a group consisting of both Roman Catholics and evangelicals issued a widely reported document entitled, *Evangelicals and Catholics Together: The Christian Mission in the Third Millennium*. It advanced the view that Catholics and evangelicals are one in Christ, and should work together as such. Especially startling to John was to find his friend, Jim Packer, prominent in the endorsements of what became known as ECT. Dr Packer, in 1988, had contributed the first Foreword to *The Gospel According to Jesus*. Packer's books were enthusiastically reviewed and promoted by Grace Church. In John's opinion,

'Few in our generation have been more effective advocates of Reformation theology than Dr Packer.'

In a Grace to You letter of June 1994, MacArthur expressed his disagreement with ECT, and set forth the Roman Catholic teaching clearly. The promoters of ECT proceeded on the basis that evangelicals and Catholics are equally to be regarded as Christians, but what makes a person a Christian was necessarily left unstated—necessarily because, according to Catholic belief, every baptised person is a Christian. And belief in baptismal regeneration rested on the foundational Roman Catholic error, namely that Scripture alone is not to be regarded as the one source of saving revelation: 'Both Scripture and Tradition must be accepted and honoured with equal sentiments of devotion and reverence.'[5]

MacArthur concluded, 'While there are some matters of our faith that are open to discussion—issues that many godly men disagree on—the means of salvation is not one of them.' He was taking this up, he said, 'out of love for Christ and His church'. No mention was made of Packer. But when later that year he published *Reckless Faith,* which contained a lengthy chapter on ECT, brief mention was unavoidable for Packer was continuing to support ECT and wrote in *Christianity Today* (Dec. 1994) 'I signed it because those who love the Lord must stand together.'

Along with others, the two men met at a private meeting in Fort Lauderdale, Florida, in January 1995. No accord could be reached and MacArthur, with R. C. Sproul and D. James

---

[5] *Catechism of the Catholic Church* (London: Chapman, 1994), p. 25. In *Reckless Faith: When the Church Loses Its Will to Discern* MacArthur addressed the ECT proposals courteously but firmly. It remains one of his most important books.

Kennedy, proceeded to a televised discussion. The discussion condemned ECT while seeking to present the motives of the evangelicals with whom they disagreed in the best possible light. But it was the end of all public co-operation with former friends. During that broadcast MacArthur said:

> I am convinced that this is only the beginning of a rather large movement which is going to continue to escalate, primarily because of the reigning cry for tolerance, because of the abysmal lack of discernment in the church and because of the tremendous impetus that this unity mentality has.[6]

Once again MacArthur was taking an unpopular position. In the face of materialistic secularism, the idea had wide support that it was time to leave aside minor differences and unite around 'mere Christianity'—a phrase used by C. S. Lewis, who was now becoming almost an evangelical icon.

As John anticipated, opposition would gather around the charge of lack of love. Under a heading, 'Pastor Blasts Trend of Goodwill Between Protestants and Catholics', the *Los Angeles Times* (March 11, 1995) deplored the position of the pastor of Grace Church. In the course of the year Grace to You offered free copies of the two tapes entitled 'Irreconcilable Differences' and 'Reckless Faith'. In a subsequent newsletter, the preacher commented, 'The response was one of the most striking in the twenty-five-year history of Grace to You.' While most were appreciative and thanked him for 'standing firm', several were not:

---

[6] The program was made available by Grace to You, entitled 'Irreconcilable Differences' and has a running time of 135 minutes. I have written more fully of this controversy in *Evangelicalism Divided: A Record of Crucial Change in the Years 1950-2000* (Edinburgh: Banner of Truth, 2000), chapter 8.

I was not so much surprised by critical responses as I was saddened. It says volumes about the times in which we live when speaking the truth on an issue as central to our faith as the means of salvation, is labelled 'bashing' or divisive.

One group of correspondents he found particularly encouraging:

You'll be interested to know many of the positive letters have come from people who were raised Catholic, and were saved only after years of holding to a works-centred system of salvation.

When MacArthur came to have closer contact with Italy, the country at the centre of Roman Catholicism, his concern over ecumenical influence at home only deepened.

John MacArthur's many visits overseas in the 1990s promoted his eagerness to help evangelicals in foreign countries with literature in their native languages. By 2010 there were few major language groups into which he had not been translated. Items were available in Korean (57 titles), Romanian (52), French (51), Russian (45), German (44), Portuguese (25), Italian (17), and Chinese (10). Several lesser-known languages have also seen translations, from Afrikaans and Albanian to Norwegian and Nepali—the last named having only his *Charismatic Chaos* (possibly the most widely circulated of all his titles). In all, thirty-five countries have been served with translations, while India and the Philippines have had special printings in English.

The main translation project in these years was that of the *MacArthur Study Bible*. In 2002 it came out in Germany;[7] in

---

[7] Christliche Literatur-Verbreitung.

2004 there were editions in Russian[8] and Spanish;[9] in 2006 in Italian[10] and French. The launching of the French edition was particularly memorable. It took place in the twelfth-century cathedral of St Peter in Geneva, at the end of a Reformation Tour in September 2006. With others on that tour, MacArthur had visited Luther's room in the Wartburg Castle, been in the reformer's pulpit at Wittenberg, and seen Zwingli's Zurich. But perhaps no sight did he admire more than the Reformation Wall at Geneva, a monument depicting the figures of Calvin, Farel, Beza, and Knox, all with their hands clasped to their Bibles. The publishers of the French *MacArthur Study Bible,* Société Biblique de Genève, had secured Calvin's pulpit for the occasion of the launching. MacArthur's sermon was from Psalm 19, showing that the message is to be 'God's word alone and nothing is to be mixed with it'. A few of his hearers that day were English-speaking tourists. Most were French speakers, who listened to simultaneous translation and, at the end, rushed 'with tears in their eyes', to purchase the Bibles which were available on the steps outside. In the words of one observer, Steve Esmond, 'It was a stunning end to the service.'[11]

While many other publishers were of course involved in the program of MacArthur's books in English and in translation, the involvement of Grace to You, backed by MacArthur, was essential. It reflected the priority he urged on Christians at home:

---

[8] Slavic Gospel Association.

[9] Editorial Portavoz.

[10] Società Biblica di Ginevra.

[11] The publishing of a Bible with explanatory notes has a noble tradition going back to the Geneva Bible of 1560; even so, the present writer has misgivings lest the authority of the text of Scripture be confused with that of the notes, however good the latter may be.

Unlike television, books freeze thoughts on the printed page, forcing us to argue, and judge ideas using our active, engaged minds. Books are permanent, requiring a response from the mind. They help us raise our thoughts and think outside ourselves and our everyday lives. It's no accident God's chosen vehicle for his special revelation was a book!

MacArthur's many overseas visits led to a consequence that no one had anticipated. We have noted how on his first visits to Russia he heard pleas for prayer that God would raise up preachers. This call was to be repeated almost wherever he went. The need was connected with the absence in many places of effective means for the preparation of students for the gospel ministry. MacArthur had never doubted that 'preachers need to go to college as well as to Calvary'. He did not mean college simply in the academic sense. In the interview with Victor Ryaguzov of Samara, already quoted, MacArthur was asked: 'How important is theological training?' to which he replied:

It is vitally important, but it must be kept in proper biblical perspective. The right kind of theological training is applied discipleship, not merely academic classroom exercises. That is why our seminary is located on our church campus, and I've always sought to keep theological training in the context of church life. The purpose of theological training is to make us better disciples and more effective ministers, not to gain academic respectability in the eyes of the world.

At this point help from the Master's Seminary came into the picture. In the twenty years after it's establishment in 1987, between eight hundred and one thousand men had been trained. A matter of particular thankfulness was the fact that, while theological seminaries across the States were said to prepare no more than fifty per cent of their students for the gospel ministry, in the first ten years of the Master's Seminary history over ninety per cent of its men went into pastorates or missionary service.

The discussions which John had with such men as Victor Ryaguzov led to a vision for training centres in foreign countries. It came to fulfilment as such agencies came to be established at Samara, Russia; Acireale in Sicily; Polokwane and Pretoria (Grace School of Ministry) in South Africa. At all these places the provision of men from the Master's Seminary played a necessary part. By 2009 twenty graduates of the Master's Seminary, along with Grace Community Church missionaries, were ministering in South Africa. One of them is Joel James, who came in 1994 and pastors Grace Fellowship, Pretoria (one of two congregations formed after John MacArthur's visits). At Grace School of Ministry in 2009 there were students from eight different countries, seven of them in Africa. One of the instructors is Dr Wayne Mack who, after teaching at the Master's Seminary and the Master's College, responded to the need in Pretoria when he was seventy years of age.

There was one factor in the way that Grace to You carried the Word of God from Sun Valley across the world in multiple languages that was not surprising to the preacher. 'How do you translate into other languages and cultures?', MacArthur was once asked by an interviewer. His reply repeated what lies at the heart of his ministry:

That has never been an issue, because if you teach the Bible it transcends every border, every language, every culture. It is as relevant today, and will be tomorrow, as in all the years since God put it down.

13

A Basket of Letters

*W*hen visiting Grace to You I have had opportunity to browse among the many letters which regularly come in. Often they contain words of personal testimony which are the more valuable because they were never intended for publication. They illustrate the truth of what MacArthur wrote in a letter to supporters in November 2003:

> I think you know the heart of Grace to You isn't finances or impressive statistics. Bible-centred resources change lives as men and women who use them grow in their understanding of God.

There is no uniformity with regard to the age or background of the correspondents. A number are young. A thirteen-year-old girl wrote:

> I'm about a two-year-old Christian—still very much a babe in Christ. But through your book, *Drawing Near,* I am growing and understanding the Bible. Reading the Bible really brings me joy! Through it, Jesus really shows me my sins, and I'm glad He is merciful to forgive me.

'I am twenty-six years old', writes a young man from Omaha, 'and I realize that I have been raised in an era of "baby" preaching and weak doctrine. I am so thankful for your program and I pray God continues to speak through you.'

The comment of the youngest that I saw was from a five-year-old, although not written by him but reported by his father:

> My five-year-old son and three-year-old daughter were fighting the other day. My wife told them to go and think about what God would want them to do to get along better. A few minutes later my son had the answer: 'Listen to more John MacArthur', he said!

Letters come from all parts of the world and all kinds of situations. A listener in Austria said: 'I am so grateful that I found you on the Internet (my son did, actually). Your series on "The Disciples' Prayer" radically changed my attitude towards prayer and the way I used to pray.' A woman in Germany wrote: 'I was nearly brought to despair looking for solid scriptural food in today's anything-goes Christianity. I want to say a heartfelt thanks for your dedication and hard work.'

A man from near Philadelphia whose twenty-six-year-old wife had recently died from lung disease, leaving three infants, wrote:

> My father gave me one of your sermons dealing with trials. I began listening to Grace to You and slowly began understanding God's love to us. God has used your teaching to guide me through the darkest days and hours of my life.

From Venezuela a man reported: 'I make a point of listening to your broadcast every chance I get, and I take vigorous notes so that I can share these studies with others in my church. Gracia a Vosotros [is helping] mould and shape our spiritual lives.' A Filipino, working in Saudi Arabia, wrote to say, 'Mr John, your web site is a great blessing for me, and I know many here are also blessed by your ministry.' The same news came from Iraq where, in a letter reporting his daily listening to Grace to You on the internet, a US Army lieutenant added, 'If you could forward this to John so he can know that he is reaching and blessing soldiers in Iraq, I would appreciate it.'

Correspondents often refer to the particular subjects that helped them. Another US service man in Iraq said: 'Your commitment to telling the truth of God's Word and not compromising that truth has been used of God to build me up in times of trouble.' The sinfulness of sin was a subject on which numbers commented. The way he addressed one particular sin, drew this memorable letter from a woman:

> I was saved in 1999 from a homosexual lifestyle. I left that life behind me and have not looked back. I do, however, still feel guilty at times. About a year after I got saved, I began attending the church my whole family attends. The pastor is well acquainted with my family and knows my background. In the seven years I attended that church, I never heard that a homosexual could be saved. They mocked and made fun of homosexuals, but that was about it. I left that church a year ago and have been listening to you every day for almost a year. I listened to your message titled, 'What God Thinks of Homosexuals', and I just cried when I heard you say God loves homosexuals, and they can be saved. I have to tell you how much your daily broadcasts have helped me grow.

A woman from Portsmouth, Virginia, wrote:

Countless times the Holy Spirit has ministered to me through your broadcast. I thank God for you. On one occasion in particular, when you were on the subject of false prophets, God really used you to bless me with His wisdom and understanding. You see, I was in the midst of a church at that time where there were indeed some of the false prophets spoken of in the Bible. After much prayer, and God speaking to me through Scripture and in my quiet time, your broadcast confirmed to me God's revelation.

Several letters speak of new understanding gained on the subject of assurance. A couple from Fresno, California, wrote:

My husband and I thank God for putting on your heart the 'Doctrines of Grace' series. It has literally changed our lives. We have prayed and prayed that God would give us assurance of our salvation . . . Only eternity will show the huge impact this series has had and is having on other folks like us who have been seeking assurance of their salvation.

A man of forty-two years recounts how, after being a nominal believer, he had recently received Christ. But

many little temptations to doubt persisted and I longed to understand the truth of His words and to glorify Him. Then one day I happened to turn on WFCU and I heard you speak. I could not believe what began to happen. You made the Word of God come alive in my mind, and you slowly peeled back forty-two years of questioning and doubt. I am still very human but Satan has lost.

A broadcast series on the sovereign grace of God and election drew a number of comments. 'Thank you from the bottom of my heart', wrote a man from Buffalo, NY. 'Listening to Pastor John stand on God's Word as he preached on election was both humbling and encouraging, and it fills me with grateful thanks.' Another wrote: 'Your sermons on election and God's sovereignty have totally changed my perspective on salvation.' As this broadcast series began, a student at Palm Beach Atlantic University wrote to say how relevant it was to discussions going on among them:

> Recently the topic of Calvinism came up. I simply want to thank you for tackling this subject. As you can imagine, I'll be listening to these podcasts on my iTunes daily, along with my roommate and other college dorm mates. Thank you, John, for your example and your unwavering commitment to the clear truth of Scripture.

Pastors and Christian workers often speak of the help they have received to give to others. With MacArthur's help, one man was able to teach a weekly Bible study through Romans to fifty Japanese nationals in Tokyo. Another engaged in prison ministry, and leading about eighty-five men in a Bible Study group, expressed his gratitude for the 'better understanding of God's Word' he had gained by the ministry of Grace to You. He also spoke of how the *MacArthur Study Bible* was being widely used among the men in the penitentiary.

A prison inmate in Ohio wrote:

> The studies on Grace to You have helped me grow in the faith a great deal. You've helped me to learn to study and maintain the integrity of the Word of God. There have been times when the messages were so convicting I almost turned them off the radio, but the Holy Spirit bore witness to the facts. I'm glad I did listen. I have seen a major change in my life over the past two years that has come by the grace of God.

From a woman in Wisconsin came these words:

It has been eighteen months since leaving a worldwide cult. Grace to You tapes, books, and radio programs have been instrumental in building my relationship with Jesus Christ, helping me to understand what it means to be saved by grace alone, and to love and serve others.[1]

A Baptist pastor from Kansas testified how the Bible preaching had widened his vision of things: 'You know how we "Baptists" are about non-Baptist churches. Well, let me say, these days are over, Grace Community Church has made the difference.'

From Arkansas a pastor wrote:

Recently I read your books *The Gospel According to the Apostles* and *The Gospel According to Jesus*. I have always had trouble with the easy-believism taught today in most evangelical churches, yet I could never put my finger on the specific problem with it. Your teaching on salvation has helped me tremendously. I have been sharing what I have been learning with my wife. Recently I preached my first message where I began to explain that salvation is more than believing a few facts about Jesus. I took my congregation through 1 John 1-2. They were amazingly silent, yet they were listening intently.

A very similar letter came from Tennessee:

I am the pastor of a small, rural, African-American church. But I found the principles you shared in your book, *Hard to Believe,* to be of universal significance to the Christian church. As a matter of fact I incorporated these teachings into our Wednesday night Bible study. We all discovered that there is a high cost to following Jesus . . . I realize that God is worthy of all the glory, but I thank you for allowing Him to reach our congregation through you.

[1] This letter and the previous one were quoted in a Grace to You letter.

A Roman Catholic priest writes from New Orleans, to tell MacArthur how he had come to know Christ as Lord and Saviour ten years earlier, fourteen years after his ordination to the priesthood:

> Since then I have become 'addicted' to Sacred Scripture. I have been listening to your radio broadcast for about five years now. I have all your study guides and several of your books and pamphlets . . . Last week I was invited to be the speaker at a Jesuit retreat on the banks of the Mississippi. I based my talks (eleven, thirty-minute talks) very heavily on your book *The Gospel According to Jesus*. There were 111 men in attendance. The director of the Retreat House told me that in all the time he had been there, he had not heard such praise for and enthusiasm about the talks.

This correspondence also reveals that it is by no means only Christians who listen to the broadcasts. Not infrequently unbelievers listen without intending to do so. A woman was listening to Grace to You when her husband came in unexpectedly for lunch. As he was very antagonistic to the gospel, her initial reaction was to turn the radio off so that he would not become angry, but something kept her from doing that. He began to listen, was gripped by the Word of God, and started to listen to Grace to You daily. Within two weeks he came home and told his wife that he had trusted the Lord Jesus as his Saviour.

A man from Michigan was raised in a Muslim family, and after the death of his father and a period of rebellion and drugs, he started to seek God:

> I started my journey in a mosque. I went there many times to ask for literature and to pray. Every time I went I felt more of a void. I was disgusted with my life and felt I was the lowest of all men . . . One day I was driving and heard

something about Christ on the radio, and I sensed I was being drawn to God. I cannot explain it—I just knew I was being drawn. I remember telling God something significant: I called Him 'Lord'. This was significant to me because Muslims never call our God 'Lord'. I promised the Lord I would go to church, which I did, and I started reading the Bible. At some time—I don't know when—I was born again by the grace of God, and I was baptized . . . I hope to become a pastor. I love listening to Grace to You—I'm comforted by your messages. My family and I are persecuted a lot, especially by other relatives. We will not bend in our faith. We live by the Word of God and are not ashamed.

A forty-three-year old black American from Tennessee wrote of how he had turned away from Christianity under the influence of the Black Power movement.

I bought into the teaching against a 'white' Jesus, and the pro-Black teachings became my religion . . . When I first heard you on radio about nine years ago, I thought to myself, 'I really don't like this guy and what he is saying.' I was pretty sure you were white. Then one day I heard you preach on forgiveness of sins and love, and the veil was lifted from my eyes. Up until then, I had never truly heard the gospel preached, never truly understood the holiness of God. The Word of God began to have an incredible impact on me as I listened to your preaching daily. By God's grace, I've been living for Him, studying His Word, and listening to your broadcast for the last nine years.

Perhaps the most important subject in all these letters has not yet been mentioned. I find it repeated in many places, and it is more closely connected with the influence of this ministry than can be estimated in this world. I refer to such comments as these: 'I keep you in my prayers daily Dr MacArthur'; 'I am praying always that our God will continue to shower you with wisdom and goodness'; 'I continue to give you my prayers and support'; 'My family is praying for your ministry.'

The Apostle Paul needed the intercession of Christian people for his work, and so do all faithful men. 'My people pray for me', was Spurgeon's comment on the fruitfulness of his work. The blessing of God on the preaching of John MacArthur is a testimony to the God who hears and answers prayer.[2]

One final thought is also too important to miss. There are no pressured appeals for money from Grace to You. Yet the work could not continue without the numbers of those who share in the ministry by their giving. Among the consequences of that support has been the opportunity it gives of extending help to those of very limited resources. It has been moving for me to read the gratitude of such individuals—ranging from pastors in small churches, to men in penitentiaries. Such words as the following are not uncommon: 'My family has been very blessed by the free resources we have received.' 'How do I say thanks for such kindness? Thank you, thank you, thank you.'

---

[2] While preparing these pages in Britain, where MacArthur has been broadcasting six days a week since 1987, a young man told me of how, at the age of fifteen, John MacArthur's preaching led to his conversion. I heard of a man of 101 years, long unaccustomed to evangelical preaching, who had come to listen every Sunday night. His funeral took place on the day I typed these words. A Christian widow, whom we often visit, makes it a practice to stop everything at 7 pm each evening to listen to MacArthur teaching the truth. Who can say how many thousands of such stories might be repeated?

An incident illustrates how Grace to You seeks to operate. A woman wrote to say she had been a listener for nearly ten years, but, while she continued to be blessed by listening, she would no longer be able to send financial support. Her husband had recently suffered a stroke. On behalf of John, a staff member called her 'to pass on a word of encouragement, and to make certain she continued to request the free books or tapes offered'. She seemed surprised a ministry would want to do this for someone unable to give.

Those who have supported this ministry have not served Christ in vain.

14

Objections and Questions

There is no shortage of examples of hostility to John MacArthur's ministry. Some of these arrive in letters to Grace to You. A lady from Utah, after hearing about his book, *The Gospel According to Jesus* on her car radio, went to the only Christian bookshop in her area:

> The man that manages the bookstore told us he was not carrying the book and he was sure he did not want to order it for us or sell it to us. Then he gave us a long speech why he didn't like MacArthur and why we shouldn't read his books.

Another man told how he had been a Christian for thirty-five years, and how listening to Grace to You was 'an outstanding resource' in his daily Christian life. But when nominated to join the board of elders in his church, an interview with the elders followed and proved a painful experience:

> I was shocked that for the first thirty minutes they trashed your ministry—as if listening to Grace to You, or reading your books, were the unpardonable sin. The elders are wanting to move toward a seeker-sensitive format.

There are different ways of explaining this kind of reaction to MacArthur's ministry, ranging from misunderstanding and misinformation, to ignorance and plain antipathy to biblical teaching.[1] I do not mean to address such generalities here, but to take up a few particular questions or objections that have not appeared in the preceding pages.

Some object not so much to the content of his preaching but to the way he says it. A pastor in Brazil complains, 'Most of the time MacArthur is rather forceful in his views and lacks cordiality toward those who disagree with him.' By way of reply it has to be agreed that MacArthur is considerably more forceful and direct than is common in contemporary preaching. He believes that if a preacher does not have authority behind what he says he should not be speaking at all in the name of God. This is the more necessary in a day when plain speaking is not 'politically correct' and, if some are put off, it is the very thing that many recognize as greatly needed. 'I was astonished at your boldness in preaching the Word', writes a listener in Florida. 'It was so refreshing. I rarely am convicted by the teaching at my church.' Others who listen to him regularly understand that, far from being indifferent to their feelings, his directness shows the opposite. A hearer writes:

> I just want to say thank you for your willingness to tell the truth regardless of how it may make us feel. The hard messages may hurt at the time but in the end lead to life and a true relationship with God. My heart is moved by your concern and evident love for people like me.

[1] Those who understand what MacArthur is teaching can generally interpret the opposition. One correspondent wrote: 'You have proven that a church can grow without a bus ministry. You have proven that folks can get saved without an aggressive altar call. You have proven that the Bible can effectively be taught without the King James Version. It is no wonder that many fanatical fundamentalists don't like you.'

Further, while MacArthur does not think a cordial attitude is appropriate towards those who are opponents of the truth, he never demeans such individuals. Probably millions have heard him on 'Larry King Live', one of America's most popular talk-shows, when he is the only Christian participant in a group discussion. The manner of his testimony on those occasions has been both definite and humble. In the words of one observer,

> It is refreshing to see the respect that Larry had for you because you stand for something and don't back down. You also show great respect for others, and that is a marvellous testimony.

Some criticism of John MacArthur comes from men who are thankful for his evangelical leadership while expressing differences. I am thinking of such men as Dr Samuel Waldron, who has opposed MacArthur on a secondary point of doctrine yet can speak of him as 'one of my modern-day heroes. I love John MacArthur and thank God for his ministry.'[2]

It is sometimes complained that John produces young preachers who seek to be replicas. That imitations may exist is not to be denied, but that he 'breeds' them is no more true than it was in the case of such men as Spurgeon and Lloyd-Jones.

Numbers of men who loved the preaching at Spurgeon's Metropolitan Tabernacle themselves went on to build 'Tabernacles', not 'churches'; and, more curiously, some admirers of Lloyd-Jones could ease their collar with a finger as accurately as they saw done in the pulpit of Westminster Chapel. But young men need leaders, and if they follow them too closely the fault is one that, with time, hopefully they will unlearn. No

---

[2] Samuel E. Waldron, *MacArthur's Millennial Manifesto: A Friendly Response* (Owensboro, KY: RBAP, 2008), p. 145.

one should be imitated. The command, 'Put not your trust in princes' (*Psa*. 146:3), rests on a good reason: in MacArthur's words, 'Throughout history God has used imperfect vessels, "that the excellency of the power may be of God and not of us" (*2 Cor*. 4:7).'

There is no ideal mould or template from which God produces others. No two men have identical gifts and there is imperfection in the best. It may well be that young men, especially graduates of the Master's Seminary, have sought to reproduce Grace Community Church, but it is unreasonable to put the blame at MacArthur's door. He wants a rising generation of preachers who uphold the principles he has taught, where they see them in the Word of God; but he does not want imitative disciples. 'Let every man prove his own work,' is the biblical principle (*Gal*. 6.4). Every man has to honour God in whatever circumstances He appoints. 'Do not be called masters', is the abiding command of Christ (*Matt*. 23:10).

Another complaint was put to MacArthur by Victor Ryaguzov when the two men were in conversation in Russia: 'Some suggest that it is your desire to break up existing denominations in foreign countries and form new ones. What is your response to this?' He replied:

It's not true. If I had any interest in trying to form a denomination, I would have done it years ago. That's not something anyone would want to undertake after spending more than forty years trying to strengthen as many denominations, associations, and fellowships as possible by helping them prepare leaders for their churches. That is still the approach to ministry I am committed to.

Nor would I ever have any interest in trying to break up existing denominations overseas. In fact, I have been openly critical of American evangelicals who have gone to Russian-speaking parts of the world and started their own churches and para-church ministries rather than making themselves servants to the churches that are already ministering there.

It could be added to this response that neither MacArthur, nor his helpers, give prominence to the work in which they are engaged. Had it been otherwise this would not have been a first published biography. And MacArthur is careful never to give the impression that he is engaged in something uniquely different from the service of many other servants of Christ. As he wrote to supporters of Grace to You (May 15, 2008):

> Grace to You is far from alone—many other ministries like ours still faithfully open God's Word every day to their audiences, both here in the United States and around the world. Some of the oldest, strongest ministries in Christian radio have been teaching the Bible for generations and are seeing more fruit from their ministries than ever.

Another critical observation sometimes raised has to do with a seemingly uncritical acceptance of a multiplication of musical instruments in public worship. This modern development has, of course, not originated with Grace Community Church or with the students of the Master's Seminary; the fault—if it be a fault—is that no check is offered to the phenomenon that has become so widespread.

In response to this, a distinction has to be made between the general subject of worship and musical instruments in particular. On the general subject MacArthur is by no means silent. It prompted his book, *The Ultimate Priority: Worship,* in which he identified neglect of God's holiness as a lack that is 'eating at the heart of our worship'. He recognizes that worship is no secondary issue: 'I am convinced that the downgrading of worship, Scripture, and theology will ultimately usher in serious doctrinal compromise.'[3] It is the lost consciousness of the majesty of God which has turned worship into what appeals to congregations:

> Perhaps the most visible signs of pragmatism are seen in the convulsive changes that have revolutionized the church worship service in the past decade. Some of evangelicalism's largest and most influential churches now boast Sunday services that are designed purposely to be more rollicking than reverent.[4]

In a treatment entitled, 'With Hearts and Minds and Voices', he gives a full and balanced survey of Christian praise, past and present, which needs to be much better known. Central to his treatment is the following conviction:

> There is certainly nothing wrong with the simple, straightforward personal praise that characterizes the best of today's praise choruses. Neither is there anything wrong with the evangelistic and testimonial thrust of yesterday's gospel songs. But it is a profound tragedy that in some circles, only contemporary choruses are sung. Other

[3] *Ashamed of the Gospel,* p. 44.
[4] Ibid., p. xiii.

congregations limit their repertoire to hundred-year-old gospel songs. Meanwhile, a large and rich body of classic Christian hymnody is in danger of being utterly lost out of sheer neglect . . .

Like it or not, today's songwriters are teachers, too. Many of the lyrics they are writing will soon be far more deeply and permanently ingrained in the minds of Christians than anything they hear their pastors teach from the pulpit. How many songwriters are skilled enough in theology and Scripture to qualify for such a vital role in the catechesis of our people?

The question is answered by the paucity of expression found in the most popular modern praise chorus—especially when compared to some of the classic hymns. Compare the lyrics of 'Shine, Jesus, Shine' with 'O Worship the King, All Glorious Above.' Or compare 'Something Beautiful' with 'O Sacred Head, Now Wounded'. I chose those examples not because I see anything erroneous or anti-biblical in those particular modern praise choruses, but because they are the best of the genre.[5]

But turning from the content of praise to musical instruments in particular, John offers little criticism, although he points out a major source of the change that has come about in this area. He quotes the 'prophecy' of James Ryle that 'God is getting ready to anoint Christian musicians with the same anointing that was given to the Beatles.' The same man attributes to God the words, 'I had a purpose, and the purpose was to usher in the charismatic renewal with musical revival around the world.'[6] This can pander to the taste of people who 'are often more concerned about

[5] John MacArthur, Joni Eareckson Tada, Robert and Bobbie Wolgemuth, *O Worship The King* (Wheaton, IL, Crossway, 2000), pp. 1-7, 12-13.
[6] *Charismatic Chaos*, p. 72.

whether they like the music than they are about whether they are hearing the truth'.[7] However, provided the intention is not to entertain or promote emotion, whether churches choose to use an orchestra, or a band, is seen by MacArthur as a question of style to be decided by local circumstances and preferences. The church, it is said, should not impose limitations where Scripture itself allows liberty. And if God approved the use of many instruments in the temple worship, why should we be more restrictive? So while any music employed in worship simply as entertainment is censured, it is said 'a music ministry' may have a subordinate place 'if it sees the ministry as a means to strengthen the church family spiritually or extend the reach of the gospel'.[8]

Personally I hope the argument that liberty is permissible, when it comes to the use of musical instruments, is one to which Dr MacArthur may give more attention. I believe the defence of musical instruments rests on the same argument that was used by opponents of the Reformers to defend the continuance of practices prevalent in the Church of Rome—from musical instruments to vestments. The defence was that if the Old Testament sanctioned these, why should they now be put aside? The answer of the Reformers and Puritans was to affirm the great change introduced by the work of Christ and the outpouring of the Holy Spirit. The temple in old Jerusalem is no longer a model for an age when everywhere there is worship 'in spirit and in truth' (*John* 4:23), when believers enter into 'the holiest of all', when Levite choirs stand down, and all sing who have 'the word of Christ' and are being 'filled with the Spirit' (*Eph.* 5:18-18; *Col.* 3:16). The New Testament church knows nothing

---

[7] *Truth War,* p. 178.
[8] *Ashamed of the Gospel,* p.183.

of temple choirs, incense, and musical instruments, because it has no need of them. To bring them back, the Reformers argued, was to take the church back to infancy.[9]

In the Reformed tradition, the use of one musical instrument, simply to set the tune, is a very different thing from introducing a collection of instruments as a part of worship, as in the Temple: a single instrument may belong to *adiaphora*, or 'things indifferent', no more to be regarded as a part of worship than the pulpit on which the preacher stands.

I entirely agree with MacArthur's statement: 'I believe worship is the church's highest priority.'[10] But, as the use of instruments is so much involved in the contemporary change taking place in the worship of many churches, I do not think it can be passed over. I might also add that the singing at a communion service at Grace Community Church, without any kind of musical accompaniment, is among the most uplifting I have heard anywhere in the world.

[9] Calvin, for example, wrote: 'Instrumental music is not fitter to be adopted into the Public Worship of the Christian Church, than the incense, the candlesticks, and the other shadows of the Mosaic law . . . Instrumental music was only tolerated on account of the times and of the people, because they were as boys. But in Gospel times we must not have recourse to these, unless we wish to destroy the evangelical perfection, and to obscure the meridian light which we enjoy in Christ our Lord' (on *1 Sam.* 18:1-9). This argument was not novel to the sixteenth century; on the contrary, it is found in the early church Fathers and explains why musical instruments in worship were 'not earlier than the eighth, and not in general use till the thirteenth century'. Even Thomas Aquinas (c. 1226-74) wrote: 'The Church does not use musical instruments to praise God lest she should seem to Judaise.' Quotations from *The Organ Question: Statements by Dr Ritchie and Dr Porteous, with Introductory Notice by Robert S. Candlish* (Edinburgh: Johnstone and Hunter, 1856), pp. 109-23.

[10] *Ashamed of the Gospel*, p. 188.

A final area where criticism has arisen needs to be touched on. On the subject of Dispensationalism MacArthur has faced opposition from opposite directions. First, from fundamentalist dispensationalists who took *The Gospel According to Jesus* as an attack on Dispensationalism, as already noted. But criticism has also come from Reformed Christians who, while admiring his ministry as a whole, regard his thinking as defective on this subject. When, for instance, preachers in Brazil were asked to note his influence on their ministries, negative comment on Dispensationalism was sometimes mentioned. 'Negatively', one wrote, 'I believe that he exemplified the possibility (I am not speaking here of consistency) of being soteriologically reformed and dispensational at the same time.' Another reported:

> John MacArthur's ministry has mostly impacted my life through literature and the academic accomplishments of the Master's College. I became familiar with MacArthur's books during the first years of my ministry in a rural congregation. A couple of books that provided a great pastoral help for my pastoral ministry during those years were *Keys to Spiritual Growth* and *Charismatic Chaos*. Later on, the work, *The Gospel According to Jesus* was very helpful in a personal struggle against prosperity theology, though the book was not written with that topic in view. As I read these books I could observe how MacArthur approached biblical passages in an expository way, and it was a great incentive to do the same (though my greatest influence in this came from D. Martyn Lloyd-Jones). However, as I kept on reading MacArthur's works, I became very disappointed with his dispensational emphasis.[11]

---

[11] These comments were acquired and translated for me by Dr Solano Portela whose tribute to John MacArthur I have already quoted above.

Perhaps the explanation why some criticize MacArthur for being no dispensationalist at all, while others say that he emphasizes it too much, lies in differing definitions of the word. If Dispensationalism means all that such authors as Scofield and Chafer have taught, then the preacher at Grace Community Church is no dispensationalist. But on his own definition of the word, John can say: 'I have not abandoned Dispensationalism, nor do I intend to.'[12]

The difference between MacArthur and what he calls 'traditional Dispensationalism' has to do with his denial of the error which puts Israel 'under law' and the church 'under grace'. The Jews were never 'under law' as a means of salvation, but all men are responsible to the unchanging law of God, including Christians, as already considered above.[13] Yet the course of future events, as believed by dispensationalists, he also believes—namely, the 'rapture' of the church, the 'coming' of Christ (after a seven-year tribulation) to reign on earth for a thousand years (the millennium) before the last judgment. Although affirming there is only one way of salvation for Jew and Gentile, he holds that a major difference continues between the church and Israel in the purposes of God. While Gentile believers were individually elected to salvation, physical Israel is also elected:

> There are only two people [groups of human beings] elections in Scripture: Israel, an eschatological group of ethnic Israelites that will constitute the future nation who will receive the promises of God, and the Church. There's no

---

[12] The differences between the original *Scofield Reference Bible* and *The New Scofield Reference Bible* (New York: Oxford University Press, 1967), of which Charles Feinberg was one of the editors, are examined by O. Palmer Robertson, *The Christ of the Covenants* (Grand Rapids: Baker, 1980), pp. 201-27.

[13] See p. 71 above.

reason to mingle the two; or because the Church is elect, therefore, cancel Israel's election. Isaiah 45:4 calls Israel 'My elect'. . . . Israel is God's elect.[14]

This latter election will be visible to all after 'the rapture', when, it is believed, 144,000 converted Jews will be the means of preparing national Israel for her role during the reign of Christ in the millennium. A summary of this teaching can be found in *The MacArthur Study Bible* (Nashville; Word, 1997), p. 2197.

Traditional Dispensationalism supported this view of unfulfilled prophecy by asserting that 'the kingdom', promised in the Old Testament, was not established in the New Testament age; fulfilment will only be after the rapture. It was claimed that to take any other view of the Old Testament promises 'made to Israel' is to deny the 'literal' language of Scripture. How that was the case in light of the way the New Testament itself interprets the Old is hard to explain, for we learn that the promises of the new covenant are already experienced in the church (*Heb.* 8:10; 12:28, etc.); 'the tabernacle of David', which God promised to rebuild, is interpreted by the Holy Spirit as referring to the bringing in of Gentile Christians (*Acts* 15:16). So Christians of Reformed persuasion commonly believe that Jew and Gentile both enter into the same promises, being grafted into the same olive tree. John MacArthur answers this case, not by excluding the church from Old Testament promises of the future kingdom (in the manner of traditional Dispensationalism), but by arguing for a double reference for the promises: they can apply to both church and Israel, only with this qualification, that at present the kingdom is 'internal, in the hearts and minds of those who

[14] Shepherds' Conference Address, 2007, printed in Waldron, *MacArthur's Millennial Manifesto*, p. 145.

belong to Jesus Christ', whereas with the Jews in the millennium it will be a visible, 'divine earthly kingdom'. (See *New Testament Commentary; Matthew 1-7*, pp. 56, 381; ibid., *2 Corinthians*, p. 98; and note on Jeremiah 31:31-34 in *Study Bible*).

I do not want to reflect on the latter statement except to say that it seems to throw doubt on whether the correct interpretation of unfulfilled prophecy is simply a case of taking either a 'spiritual' or a 'literal' view of Scripture. The 'literal' interpretation is not necessarily the true one—a mistake the Jews made in not understanding that 'Elijah' had already come (*Matt.* 11:14), and that the kingdom of God was 'in the midst' of them (*Luke* 17:21).

While dispensational convictions are certainly to be found in John MacArthur's books, how far they are prominent is a matter of opinion. In some of his most important books they do not come in at all. While the danger of an increasing apostasy is a very real one for him, he is cautious in offering interpretations of contemporary events as the fulfilment of Scripture, and rejects the kind of sensational teaching on prophecy which has discredited the very subject.[15]

This is not the place for an extended discussion of subjects on which much has been written.[16] Certain passages in the book

---

[15] His thought has matured in this area. He would not write now, as he did in the Grace to You letter, April, 1980: 'Time is limited. As I study Ezekiel 38, I see Russia in conquering Afghanistan moving into the place of prophetic set up for the return of Jesus Christ.'

[16] From MacArthur's standpoint, much recommended reading can be found through the *Index of The Master's Seminary Journal*, vols 1-20, available on CD. Included in that source is Richard Mayhue's response to J. H. Gerstner's critique of Dispensationalism (*Journal*, Spring, 1982). From the Reformed standpoint I would recommend W. J. Grier, *The Momentous Event* (Edinburgh: Banner of Truth, 1970, often reprinted), and O. T. Allis, *Prophecy and the Church* (Philadelphia: Presbyterian and Reformed, 1945).

of Daniel, the closing chapters of Ezekiel and Zechariah, the three passages claimed to teach the 'rapture',[17] verses in Romans 11, and the manner in which the book of Revelation is to be interpreted—all these are relevant for the determination of the issues. That an important difference exists in the understanding of these and other parts of Scripture is not to be denied, and they are a reminder that we are to call no man 'Teacher'. At the same time, the words of Palmer Robertson are also important:

> It should not be forgotten that covenant theologians and dispensationalists stand side by side in affirming the essentials of the Christian faith. Very often these two groups within Christendom stand alone in opposition to the inroads of modernism, neo-evangelicalism, and emotionalism. Covenant theologians and dispensationalists should hold in highest regard the scholarly and evangelical productivity of one another. It may be hoped that continuing interchange may be based on love and respect.[18]

[17] 'The rapture is the subject of three passages in the New Testament (*John* 14:1-4; *1 Corinthians* 15:51-54; *1 Thessalonians* 4:13-17).' *John MacArthur Explains the Book of Revelation* (Chicago: Moody, 2007), p. 93.
[18] *The Christ of the Covenants*, pp. 201-2.

15

The Changing Scene in the United States

*N*ations do not stand still, and by the last decade of the twentieth century there was much evidence of moral collapse in an increasingly materialistic culture. An age had dawned in which traditional Christian values were being shunned by many in public life. 'What are Christians to do,' MacArthur asked in 1993, 'when the government allows the wholesale slaughter of babies, exalts homosexuality, and denigrates any kind of moral standard?' Answers to the situation were diverse. Some thought a public relations campaign should be a priority. Others advocated the need for more social action, and the organizing of political pressure with demonstrations and protests. There were not lacking those who thought that psychology or mysticism could aid in reversing the decline in Christian belief.

For John MacArthur such proposals were only adding to the confusion. Not the reformation of culture but the salvation of men and women is the church's mandate. But too many churches lacked a sufficient hold on truth to fulfil such a calling. They lacked the faith to assert that from Scripture

> we can understand the ebb and flow of life better than all the educators, philosophers, politicians and social pundits combined . . . A look at the trends sweeping today's churches demonstrates just how small a god we've fashioned. How else can we explain the boom in Christian psychology, flashy, Las Vegas-style worship services, and high-tech church growth seminars?

In the midst of change, MacArthur saw no need for faithful churches to change what they were already doing. If any new development was to come to the situation at large it would only be by the power of God upon the witness to Christ and His Word. By the 1990s there were signs of a hopeful new development, and on this we must now comment.

I have already noted that Fundamentalism, in which so much of evangelical witness was to be found, had broken into two branches in the 1960s: one belligerent towards any change, and the other (the 'new-evangelicalism' as it was sometimes called) anxious for status and academic respectability. MacArthur never belonged to the latter, and from the time of the Lordship controversy he had also parted from many in traditional fundamentalist circles. While some would have still identified him with Fundamentalism in the 1980s, the publication of *The Gospel According to Jesus* in 1988 made a division plain. As a consequence of this parting, he might have been left an individual, semi-isolated in a sphere of his own, had there not been a stirring that would take numbers of Christians in a new direction.

By the 1990s there were congregations, small and large, across the United States, which were hearing preaching that forty years earlier would have been hard to find. The message sounded akin to the doctrines of the Reformation and Puritan periods, but it had sprung afresh from Scripture, from the literature of those earlier periods, and was gaining surprising support from the younger generation.[1]

To call this development a 'movement' would be to misconceive it, at least in the normal use of that term. It had no particular starting point, knew no party planners, and made no public claims. Rather streams of influence had risen quietly in different places, under different men, and in different denominations, yet flowing spontaneously in the same direction. In so far as there were leaders, they were usually conspicuous as preachers, not academics, for the influence was coming from pulpits, from men who believed it was the preaching of the Word of God that always brought fresh life to the churches.

The powerful ally for these men was surprising. It was the evangelical authors of an older school, long unsought and unread, but now in print again and in many hands. In the 1950s Dr Wilbur Smith commented on the absence of the titles of Jonathan Edwards and other Puritans from all book lists. In the 1990s Edwards was not only widely available again but being read by thousands. Other authors in the same tradition—John Owen at their head—came back as though from the dead. The few contemporary writers who also contributed to this change have, for the most part, already been named in these pages.

---

[1] The resurgence of doctrinal Christianity appears to have begun quietly through books in the 1960s. George Dollar wrote in 1973; 'In the last ten years a new threat has emerged within Fundamentalism itself. This has been the militant and rigid Calvinism, usually expressed in its Five Points . . . a growing number within Baptist circles have read the English Puritans and followed Spurgeon in the persuasion that sovereign grace demands the acceptance of all of the Five Points.' *History of Fundamentalism,* p. 276. Numbers of the readers of the Puritans in the 1960s and '70s had become preachers of influence by the 1990s.

Books alone cannot bring change unless there is spiritual hunger to read them, and by the 1990s there was such hunger. Dr J. I. Packer's treatment of the attributes of God had reached a comparatively small circle when first published in England in the *Evangelical Magazine* (c. 1960); but, after being re-issued in book form in the United States in the 1970s under the title *Knowing God,* sales were to soar to approximately three million by 2005.

Only the existence of this same hunger can explain the growth and multiplication of conferences of a new kind across the United States. At these the speakers no longer majored on such themes as 'How to be Contemporary', or 'How to Build a Successful Church', but on doctrinal teaching and the exposition of Scripture. A renewed reading of history and biography was also showing how doctrinal beliefs had formerly changed the history of the English-speaking peoples. When MacArthur first held a Shepherds' Conference for pastors in 1980, the original chapel building in Sun Valley was large enough to hold the few hundred who attended; and there were few other conferences like it. But in the next twenty years such conferences multiplied across the land; they included the Philadelphia Conference, the Bethlehem Conference (at Minneapolis), the Bolton Conference in New England, the Ligonier Conference in Florida, to name only a few. Even in the Deep South, where in the Southern Baptist Convention it had been axiomatic that 'Calvinism' and evangelism could not live together, a Founders Conference was inaugurated to point the denomination back to its roots. By the end of the century Tom Ascol, editor of the *Founders Journal,* could speak of 'the extent to which the revival of the doctrines of grace is sweeping across the churches of our land'.

Although not belonging to the same denominations, the leaders of these conferences were drawn together by shared convictions. James Montgomery Boice, organizer of the Philadelphia Conference, was one of MacArthur's earliest friends from the Reformed side. He lectured at Talbot Seminary in 1979, and he preached at the Thirtieth Anniversary of MacArthur's ministry in 1999, before succumbing to an aggressive cancer the following year. Prior to Boice and Packer writing Forewords to *The Gospel According to Jesus* (1988), MacArthur has said, 'I wasn't moving in Reformed circles.' A close friendship began with R. C. Sproul when John spoke at the Ligonier Conference in 1992; it was to be the first of many such visits to Orlando, Florida. Similarly MacArthur was in Minneapolis with John Piper in 1997. In turn, Sproul and Piper came to speak at Grace Community Church.

A shared faith in the sovereignty of God also brought MacArthur among a new generation of Calvinistic men in Southern Baptist circles. One of these was Mark Dever, pastor of Capitol Hill Baptist Church, Washington DC, and another was Albert Mohler, President of The Southern Baptist Theological Seminary, at Louisville, Kentucky. When an editor of *Christianity Today* visited the bookstore of that Seminary the first books he saw were not those authored within that denomination: 'Right away I noticed a prominent display of John MacArthur's commentaries. The noted Calvinist expositor does not belong to SBC.'[2]

---

[2] Collin Hansen, *Young, Restless, Reformed, A Journalist's Journey with the New Calvinists* (Wheaton: Crossway, 2008), p. 69.

That MacArthur's ministry was very much a part of the resurgence of Reformed belief was not at first understood by all who listened to him. At the Shepherds' Conference in 1997 some of the 3,000 men present were a little surprised at things they heard. Particularly was this the case in a session at which questions were put to MacArthur without prior notification. They came freely from the floor, and the first was, 'John, you spend a lot of time with guys in the Reformers' camp, what are some of the things that attract you to them, and what are some of the differences?'

The reader of these pages is already familiar with part of the response, but we give the whole now in John's own words:

> There are a number of ways to answer that question. I have always since my days as a Seminary student been committed to Reformed soteriology.[3] People say, 'When did you become Reformed?' Well, I don't know that that is anything very recent. In my days as a student in College I was a typical football-type player, and I never let my books get in the way of my education, and just kind of went through the motions. But I always had this voracious appetite for Scripture, even as a young person. I remember at fourteen wanting to understand the deep things of God, and reading things like Thomas à Kempis, and all the books by E. M. Bounds. But I didn't really know where to go with it all; I just had this desire to know the Word of God. Even then I also read some missionary biographies which had a profound effect on me. So I was attracted to serious things with regard to the Word of God, even though I wasn't particularly serious in my personality. I was always frustrated by not understanding the Scriptures. People would say to me, 'You should read the Bible every day, take

---

[3] Soteriology: the doctrine of salvation.

fifteen minutes.' I would read it and not understand what it meant, and have to go and try and find out—asking my father or someone.

When I got into Seminary we had some extra reading to do, and our theology professor, Dr Bob Saucy channelled me towards the Princeton people—B. B. Warfield, Machen, and others. I began to read them, and found a depth of understanding of the Word of God, a depth of dealing with doctrinal issues. It was not inconsistent with what I had believed in the past, but was much more refined and deeper. So in Seminary I began to read more. I came across a book by Stephen Charnock called *The Existence and Attributes of God*. I was absolutely blown away by the fact that that guy could say so much about the existence and attributes of God. It's the kind of book you read all your life; you have to take it in small doses because it is so loaded. That appealed to me because I wanted to understand the Scripture in depth. Then I began to read Thomas Watson's *Body of Divinity*. I read it and read it and marked it up, when I was still a Seminary student, sorting through lots of things. I was drawn to people who had thought so deeply about the Word of God and that drew me to Reformed theology. It wasn't so many years after that that I got a whole set of Thomas Manton's writings. So the attraction for me to Reformed theology is not because of the system; it is because of the people, the way they dealt with the Word of God with such accuracy, and the way they were able to pull out of it such clarity of doctrine. I've never been much of a systematizer as such. I have always been committed to the fact that theology should be exegetical; and I really do believe that Reformed theology, at its heart was exegetical. When you get Calvin's Commentaries you begin to realize that the greatest of John Calvin is not his *Institutes,* the greatest is in his Commentaries, because I want to know how he treated the various passages of Scripture.

I haven't really changed but through the years my understanding of the great themes of the doctrines of grace, or Reformed theology, has been greatly refined, and it's been refined because I have been twenty-eight years expounding the Scriptures, and finding that such great theology stood the test of the text.[4]

MacArthur went on to speak briefly on elements in Reformed theology relating to eschatology and ecclesiology which he did not believe. He remains resolute in his conviction on baptism for believers only.[5]

The next question was this: 'In our local newspaper they were talking about the changing face of religion in America; and included something from a George Barna report which said, in the twenty-first century the church will increasingly become a cyber church, and there will be less and less of believers gathered together in local fellowships. I would like to get your reaction to that information.'

In reply MacArthur emphasized the seriousness of the mistake made when we allow our culture to dictate our practice—'buying into cultural formulas for ministry may take you where you

---

[4] Phil Johnson has pointed to one area where MacArthur's thinking was 'refined' in the 1990s: while the latter had always held the substitutionary nature of the atonement, Johnson believes its relationship to justification now came into sharper focus, 'He began to stress that truth regularly and expound it more thoroughly than ever before'. *Truth Endures*, p. 215. If Christ justifies all for whom He died, then the atonement cannot have been universal in its design. There was also, I believe, a fuller understanding of the nature of assurance in MacArthur's chapter contributed to *Assured by God* (2006), where he shows that a profound sense of one's sinfulness is not incompatible with true assurance, and that repentance is to be lifelong.

[5] His address, 'Baptism: The Case for Believers' Baptism', is available from Ligonier Ministries.

don't mean to go'. He instanced the effects of such ideas as those of David Watson who thought that by concentrating on the spoken word the churches were becoming irrelevant, and believed that a drama group could be more effective.[6] This issue led MacArthur back to the previous question:

There's no question that, in the future, the culturally oriented and defined church will take on the forms that the culture dictates, and it will drift off into who knows what. Here is one of the reasons why Reformed theology is booming the way it is, and it is booming. I remember that as a Seminary student I knew only one little Calvinistic church of about thirty people. But as evangelical Christianity has abandoned sound doctrine, in response there is a backlash among people who are saying, 'We cannot take this amorphous approach; we are tired of the most a-theological kind of evangelical telling us where the bottom line is.' That is basically what has happened. The 'experientialists', mostly charismatics and others as well, have determined that what is most important is that they get into mainstream acceptance, no matter how aberrant they might be; and evangelicalism thinks she needs to embrace them, accept them, not fight and be divisive. The result is an acceptance of the 'irreducible minimum', in which all are to be embraced, and any other theology is held to be 'divisive' and so forth. In that kind of amorphous, a-theological environment, people who have a real love for the Word of God are looking for somewhere to go to get some answers, and to get some substance and content, some biblical interpretation and theology on which to anchor

[6] 'Most churches rely heavily on the spoken or written word for communication, and then wonder why so few people find the Christian faith to be relevant. The truth is we live in a world that is almost dominated by drama.' David Watson, *I believe in the Church* (London: Hodder and Stoughton, 1982), p. 221.

their lives in the shifting sand. As this 'experiential' [feeling-centred] movement gets larger and larger, I believe the swing back towards Reformed theology is going to grow and grow. The movement is rapidly growing; even the Southern Baptists are trying to return to their roots in Reformed theology, as well as other groups.

And there is the development of books on Reformed theology. Much of what I write is Reformed theology basically. The book that I wrote, *The Gospel According to Jesus,* was basically Reformed theology, a statement on soteriology, and *Faith Works* was even more definitive as a statement on that.[7] I don't think people read it as that because I don't quote the *Westminster Confession*—I try to stick with the Scripture. But there is definitely a swing back, and we can hope and pray. It is still God-gifted men, preaching the Word of God expositionally and doctrinally, that is God's plan to bring in the redeemed and build the church.

Subdued silence followed this answer, to be interrupted by one or two individuals who could not refrain from clapping. 'Thank you both', MacArthur said dryly, and then, with broadening smile, 'Maybe I will say something that you will all like later in the week!' There were certainly many present who were thankful for what they had heard.

John MacArthur (as Martyn Lloyd-Jones) does not wave the labels 'Calvinist' or 'Reformed'. He wants people to be convinced by Scripture itself, not by any other authorities:

I normally prefer to avoid using the term Calvinism because it often provokes too much emotion and too many

---

[7] In a Grace to You letter of July 16, 2008, he observed: *'The Gospel According to Jesus* has helped define the ministry of Grace to You . . . In most of the places around the world where we minister God's truth, that book was the instrument the Lord used to open the doors of ministry for us.'

misconceptions to be useful if the goal is real understanding rather than merely vigorous debate.'

Instead he usually uses the term 'the doctrines of grace'. But sometimes the better-known term is unavoidable, as when in 2008 Grace to You entitled his two-part series on these doctrines, 'Hot Button Questions on Calvinism'. After endorsing a reprint of *The Five Points of Calvinism* in 2004, he was careful to add, 'I believe them, not because of their historical pedigree, but because that is what Scripture teaches.'[8] In the same book he repeated what he had said in 1997: 'The Spirit of God is moving the church to re-establish the glorious high ground of sovereign grace in salvation.'[9] It was a conviction shared by his friends. In October 2003, when Mark Dever asked R. C. Sproul to name 'the things you most appreciate about the current scene in American evangelicalism', the Presbyterian preacher replied, 'The recovery of interest in Puritanism, the recovery of concern for reformational theology.'

The ministry at Sun Valley had joined with a wider awakening to doctrinal Christianity. Far from being isolated, MacArthur's preaching and books were clearly an important part of a larger momentum and regrouping. By the first decade of the present century this turn round in belief was conspicuous enough to come to the notice of the secular press, first in *Time* magazine, and then in other journals read nationwide. It also became the

---

[8] D. T. Steele, C. T. Thomas, S. Lance Quinn, *The Five Points of Calvinism: Defined, Defended, and Documented* (Phillipsburg, NJ: P&R, 2004), p. 140.
[9] Said at 2007 Shepherds' Conference.

subject of a first book when Collin Hansen wrote, *Young, Restless, Reformed: A Journalist's Journey with the New Calvinists* (Wheaton: Crossway, 2008). Hansen, editor-at-large for *Christianity Today*, was enthusiastic about how the Calvinistic resurgence had begun to 'reclaim and reform evangelicalism'. He believed: 'Though today's Calvinists remain outnumbered, their influence leavens the evangelical movement . . . The growth of the Reformed ranks, especially among youth, portends significant changes ahead.'[10] On the Southern Baptist scene, he quotes the words of Tom Ascol, 'The International Mission Board is flooded with Calvinists.'

Hansen's book gave particular significance to the first 'Together for the Gospel' conference that took place in April 2006, as marking a new unity:

> Good friends Dever, Mahaney, Ligon Duncan, and Al Mohler, invited three of their heroes—Piper, John MacArthur, and R. C. Sproul—to join them in addressing a crowd of about three thousand pastors in Louisville, Kentucky . . . The four middle-aged Together for the Gospel hosts watched their heroes, each older than sixty, address a crowd mostly in their twenties and thirties.[11]

From all this it might be assumed that John MacArthur sees in the recovery of doctrinal Christianity the prospect of a major advance in progress. Certainly the 'booming' of Reformed theology, which he noted in 1997, has continued; and the extent of the demand for his own books and radio ministry is part of the evidence. But his thankfulness is mixed with a measure of

---

[10] *Young, Restless, Reformed*, pp. 113-14. While Hansen surveys leaders in some of the larger churches, it is his belief that 'the backbone of the Reformed resurgence comprises ordinary churches' (p. 158).

[11] Ibid., p. 107.

concern. It was reflected in his declining to be interviewed for Hansen's book.[12]

I can think of reasons for that concern. For one thing, it is premature to be confident the advance will continue. As MacArthur surveyed the first decade of the present century he knew that all was by no means bright. If ground was being won in some areas, it was still being lost in others. He noted how, to gain larger audiences, Bible teaching on radio in the United States was losing air time to 'Christian music and live talk'. A similar compromise was 'at epidemic levels among Christian publishers'. There was no end of controversy in sight. He commented in 2008:

> When I came out of Seminary I really did not expect to fight the battles I have fought. I never thought I would spend most of my life on the broader evangelical front defending the gospel and sound doctrine.

Instead of being excited at the new interest that journalists were showing in Calvinism and the Puritans, MacArthur remembers how 'promotion' of the gospel by the secular press had proved a dangerous thing in the past.[13] The kind of thing that gains the attention of the world, especially excitement over numbers and personalities, are of small consequence in the kingdom of God. 'If a thing is successful, it must be true', is a maxim that has done much harm among evangelicals and he

---

[12] Noted by Hansen, ibid., p. 145. In an article, 'The Calvinistic Resurgance in America', Erroll Hulse wrote: 'In the next edition Collin Hansen should seek again an interview with John MacArthur Jr. The ministries led by MacArthur represent a large proportion of the Calvinistic Resurgence.' *Reformation Today*, Nov.-Dec. 2008, p. 39.

[13] When the newspaper owner, William R. Hearst, gave orders to promote Billy Graham in *Time, Life,* and *Newsweek* in 1949, the results were by no means all beneficial.

does not want to see it continued. History shows clearly enough that truth is often with the remnant.

Further, while Hansen correctly says 'the backbone of the Reformed resurgence comprises ordinary churches', that is obscured by his heavy concentration on those whom he considers to be the leaders. The book looks at things far too largely on the human level, and leaves the impression of a movement of 'New Calvinists', promoted by mass meetings and celebrity preachers. But this kind of treatment is misleading.[14] A survey of the 'Hansen type' looks like something already familiar instead of something new, for evangelicalism has far too often indulged in the following of personalities. If this is indeed a recovery of Reformation belief, the Hansen presentation is out of harmony with the influence of the man who would not so much as have his name put on his grave in Geneva. Genuine Reformed faith teaches Christians to sing,

> The glory Lord, from first to last,
> Is Thine, is Thine alone.

Every genuine work of God is incapable of being adequately explained on the human level. There is mystery in it. Truth 'springs from the earth' independently of what may be happening elsewhere. In so far as a new unity has come into being today—as we believe it has—it has not come from meetings or organizations. A true revival of God-centred Christianity has

---

[14] It gives some grounds for Darryl Hart to criticize 'Hansen's description of this odd collection of Baptists, charismatics, and emergents as Calvinists'. Review entitled, 'Young Calvinism without an Edge', *Ordained Servant*, vol. 18, 2009 (Committee of the Orthodox Presbyterian Church), p. 150. MacArthur certainly does not think that all who are now being called 'New Calvinists' are sharers in a common purpose. He is openly critical of Mark Driscoll, whom Hansen treats as a leader, and certainly does not believe that Reformed and Puritan belief will lead men in the charismatic direction.

always had with it the biblical caution not to be called masters, and to cease from man. While recommending Hansen's survey, Don Carson had good reason to add:

> This is not the time for Reformed triumphalism. It is the time for quiet gratitude to God and earnest intercessory prayer, with tears, that what has begun well will flourish beyond all human expectation.[15]

In the present writer's opinion, a lesson from nineteenth-century German church history is relevant for us. Daniel Edward has written of how hope of a lasting evangelical revival in Prussia failed. 'The ten or fifteen years before 1848 spread out in bright sunshine in the remembrance of all Christians.' A galaxy of eminent teachers and preachers appeared to be turning the tide. 'They saw', Edward wrote,

> the excellence of the gospel as the divine scheme of redemption; they were strong for Christ as the only Saviour, but they rejected the law as the schoolmaster that leads to Christ. They set forth eloquently the privileges of the gospel to a people . . . who needed first of all to hear the voice, 'Repent'. . . These good men failed for want of what our forefathers styled 'law work'. They wanted a deeper knowledge of God's holy law, and a deeper knowledge of sin as the transgression of it.[16]

That lesson remains a warning for today. In the current recovery of Calvinistic thinking there is need for greater fear of God, of His majesty and holiness. Such features have ever accompanied a powerful work of the Spirit of God, and they

---

[15] Words included in endorsements on the book.
[16] 'The Course of the Church in Prussia during the present Century', *British and Foreign Evangelical Review*, vol. xxiv (London: Nisbet, 1875), pp. 700-701.

are connected with the revelation of His character as Lawgiver. There is not yet the evidence of such conviction of sin as has marked all the spiritual awakenings of history. For too long, in MacArthur's words, evangelical circles have been better at merriment than mourning. This is no argument against joy and song, but where the presence of God is felt there is also godly fear. When the Spirit of God is poured out men have better understood the text: 'The Lord is in His holy temple: let all the earth keep silence before Him' (*Hab*. 2:20).

16

A Visit to
Grace Community Church

W ell before eight o'clock on Roscoe Boulevard in Sun
Valley, cars began to turn into the car park at Grace
Community Church. It was a Sunday morning early in 2010
and we were glad to be there again. At 8 am a meeting of some
twenty elders began in a room adjacent to the main auditorium,
with John MacArthur present. After a few minutes of conversation, all fell to their knees and the best part of half an hour was
given to prayer. On this particular morning, a church member
was introduced briefly by an elder. This Christian woman had
been unwell and questioned whether the toleration of bitterness
in her heart had brought chastisement from God. Prayer was
made particularly and tenderly for her recovery.

At 8.30 morning worship began promptly, led by Clayton
Erb, Minister of Music. By that hour the main auditorium was
comfortably filled, although hundreds of the members were
elsewhere. Simultaneously with the first service, seven Fellowship meetings were taking place in various parts of the spacious

premises. They meet under the care of eight pastors (elders of the church); although not called such, these meetings almost amount to churches. Two of them are designated for 'All Ages'; one for 'Young Marrieds and Families', another for 'Junior High' (Grades 7-8); two are held in Spanish; and one is for the Mentally Disabled. The subjects being taken that morning in these Fellowships included: Studies in Characters; Sin's Genesis James 1:13-18; 1 John; and 1 Timothy. Two Sunday schools also run concurrently, one of them for the Deaf.

After a short intermission, those attending these Fellowships moved to the main auditorium where the morning service is repeated at 10:30 am, while another seven Fellowships convene under different leaders, along with another Children's Sunday School. The number in attendance at both main services is commonly about the same. With the total of people on the premises approaching 6,000, there is no possibility of all being able to be present in the main auditorium at the same time.

The Fellowships are the key to understanding how members of Grace Church are all individually known and cared for. The elders/pastors are not simply responsible for the Sunday meetings of their group, but exercise an on-going care for all who attend. A register of names is kept every week. The Fellowship at which I was present, has about four hundred regular members,[1] and an information sheet was given to all present relating to matters for prayer, the care of the home-bound, and the nine Home Bible studies meeting in different locations.

At the main service every person was welcomed at the door and given an attractive ten-page news sheet. It contained

[1] The largest of the Fellowships runs to some eight hundred members, but the majority are closer to about two hundred.

information on the services of the day, information on various meetings, book notices, and missionary news. The Conover family, Bob, Margie, and their children, were home after twenty-one years service in the Muslim world—Morocco and Jordan. Bart Horton wrote of a team of eight adults, and their children, about to leave Grace for work in Lebanon. The church currently sends and supports more than sixty missionary families, located on six continents. They are all under the oversight of Grace elders, and receive periodic visits. On this particular Sunday, I learned that one elder was absent in India, another was about to go to the United Kingdom, and a third to Russia.

Perhaps about half of the elders/pastors are full-time staff; and, seeing how the church is administered, one can understand this necessity. But much work is also undertaken by volunteers, both on Sundays and on weekdays. The early tradition of personal evangelism has been on-going; there are groups that minister in jails and detention centres, and fifty or more serve weekly at Grace to You. In one year John noted that 4,632 hours of labour had been given by such helpers. Among those helping on Sundays are John and Patricia MacArthur's now grown-up children: Matthew MacArthur teaches a sixteen-week repeated course on 'Fundamentals of the Faith'; his younger brother Mark leads a Bible Study in a Fellowship group. Their sister Marcy helps, among many services, in the Mentally Disabled Fellowship, and Melinda gives time to her very young children while aiding in the children's division of the work. These four are the parents of MacArthur's fifteen grandchildren, who are all in the church as well.

The evening service was held at 6 pm, again preceded by an elders' prayer meeting, where the number is only slightly less than in the morning. MacArthur has long called for believers to be at the worship services twice on Sundays. The auditorium was again comfortably filled, although the worshippers knew that MacArthur was recovering from a strained back and would not be preaching then as he normally does. In his place that night was an Associate Pastor who preached a telling and convicting sermon on 'Pride and Prejudice' from James 2. With far less instrumental accompaniment than in the morning services, it seemed to me the congregational singing was better in the evening. Frequently there are also baptisms during the evening service. There was none on this particular Sunday, but John has a comment on the importance of the ordinance which I will insert here. It arose out of a particular Sunday when a young mother gave her testimony at her baptism. She had come to conviction and to Christ after a car crash in which both her husband and her youngest child were killed:

> She entered our baptism pool, told of her conversion, and spoke of a loving God who is no longer a stranger. While not all our weekly baptism testimonies are so dramatic, they do have one thing in common: God's unique, custom-tailored process of bringing sinners to Himself is always clearly articulated and given a wide audience. Each of us in attendance hears first-hand the tender themes of salvation spoken from the heart of saints of every race, age, and religious background. We hear of conviction, repentance, and transformation where sin, rebellion, pain, and dissatisfaction once reigned. The once blind and dead speak of light and life. Those previously at war with God, and with no desire to know Him, humbly bow before Jesus as Lord, recognizing the unfathomable reality of sins pardoned, and the freedom, joy, and peace that comes with new life.

On the Sunday about which I have been speaking, MacArthur preached in the morning on 'The Power and Pity of Christ' from Mark 5:21-43. The course of his morning preaching had been determined way back in 1981, following the meeting with Moody Press in Chicago when they had asked for a series of New Testament commentaries. After much prayer and reflection he had agreed, believing that 'if the commentaries were well done, they could ultimately be more enduring than any other aspect of his ministry'. Plans were then settled for a project that would take ten years and be the largest ever undertaken by Moody Press. The time scale proved to be wrong, for the work was to be greater than anyone imagined in 1981. First John took longer in preaching through the New Testament books than had been anticipated. The Gospel of Matthew, for instance, needed 226 sermons. Then there was the arduous business of transferring the spoken word from recordings into written form. The process sounds straightforward; in reality the difficulty involved is one that has often prevented preachers becoming authors, speaking and writing being two very different media. While Moody's editors undertook the initial work, and put the sermons into chapters, it all had to come back to John, several chapters at a time, with the expectation that they would be returned within a month. There might then be a 'free' period until another lot arrived. He developed the habit of carrying the commentary manuscripts about with him to use spare moments on them. A note to Jerry Jenkins—Moody's initiator of the series—gives some insight into this process, as well as MacArthur's own estimate of its significance. He wrote to Jenkins on June 9, 2005:

You set in motion the history of my life! At least, in large part. Would you believe I have had to do two commentary chapters a week since the series started? At least the Study Bible was done in three intense years, and I can give further work on that to translators. The bottom line, I keep telling Patricia, is that the *New Testament Commentary* series is my most important contribution by far—so thanks!

Noting the work involved in the commentary series, Phil Johnson has recorded: 'Sometimes John goes through a chapter twice or more (if he heavily revises). So he actually edits at a rate of about two or more a week, though he might get as much as three weeks rest between chapter lots.'

The *MacArthur New Testament Commentary* thus went forward slowly. The first ten years saw *Hebrews* (1983), *1 Corinthians* (1984), *Ephesians* (1986), *Galatians* (1987) and four volumes of *Matthew* (1985-89). By December 2009, 791 chapters had been edited and published in twenty-eight volumes of the *New Testament Commentary*. Yet even this was not the whole. One more Gospel remained to be completed, namely, the series on Mark, with which the preacher was engaged on the occasion of the visit of which I have been speaking. The long-term result of the 1981 decision has thus kept MacArthur preaching through the New Testament.

Discussion of the commentary series is a suitable point at which to pause and introduce the assessment of MacArthur's preaching on Matthew given in the latest volume of Dr Hughes Oliphant Old's significant series, *The Reading and Preaching of*

the Scriptures in the Worship of the Christian Church. The reader of Old's words—which I will abbreviate—will understand that their value is limited by the short selection of sermons on which they are based. A fuller hearing or reading of the preacher would have given rise to a revision of some statements. Dr Old's theological standpoint is probably closer to contemporary Princeton than to that of Sun Valley, but if that is the case there is an added value to his assessment:

> To get a feel for the way MacArthur handles the ministry of the Word, I ordered his ten sermons on the eighth and ninth chapters of the Gospel of Matthew. The preacher has to deal with some tough questions in these two chapters. I was curious how someone with a reputation for solid expository preaching, such as MacArthur has, might interpret these passages. Listening to these sermons was a rewarding experience, even if I have a number of reservations and hesitations about MacArthur's approach to preaching.
>
> These miracles [in Matthew 8-9] were performed in Galilee, and our preacher takes the time thoroughly to set the geographical scene, giving us a vivid picture of the countryside. Many of these nine miracle stories are healing stories, and our preacher has collected an impressive amount of material not only about the diseases mentioned but also about how they were understood and treated in ancient times. Sometimes all this material is a bit ponderous, and he tells us more than we really want to know, but more often it makes for a fascinating sermon.
>
> In the way of human-interest stories one finds, on the other hand, very little. The illustrative material focuses on the biblical story. It is the passage of Scripture that is illuminated rather than a principle drawn out of the

passage. MacArthur has an amazing ability to explain Scripture by Scripture. Particularly illuminating is the way MacArthur emphasizes the similarity between Matthew and John on the one hand and Matthew and Paul on the other. He does not overburden the sermon with material that only the more initiated members of his congregation can follow, but for the more serious listener these parallel passages make the sermon richly informative and mightily convincing.

Realizing that a significant school of modern biblical scholarship has denied that Paul's elaborate theology was based on the simple gospel of Jesus, our preacher is careful to show the similarity between the two. It is very interesting to note that the polemic implied does not come to the surface. MacArthur simply shows how Paul preaches the same gospel as Matthew. One gets the impression that MacArthur is first of all an expositor and only after that a polemicist. This speaks enormously to his credit.

Having said this, however, one has to admit that our preacher has a very clear line of interpretation on these miracle stories in Matthew 8 and 9. As he sees it, these miracles are above all the proofs of Christ's divinity. They are not examples of what the power of faith can do. Much less are they the myths that symbolically express the devotion of the early Christians to their extraordinary teacher. One never gets the impression that this preacher has the least shadow of doubt but that these miracles took place exactly as they are recorded. Defending the accuracy of the Bible seems to interest MacArthur not at all. This basic assumption that the text of Scripture is reliable is part of the foundation of his effectiveness as an interpreter.

For the last couple of generations the idea that one should make the major theme of these two chapters that the miracles proved the divinity of Jesus was about the last thought an enlightened preacher would try to make. That, however, is just the point MacArthur does make. He makes the point very successfully. He shows from the structure of the text itself that this is what Matthew is trying to say. He supports it with parallel texts from both the Synoptic Gospels and the Johannine literature. What is surprising is that there is no vitriolic attack on the 'higher critics' or the 'modernists'.

The one direction in which MacArthur does let loose a moderate amount of polemic is toward the charismatics and faith healers. Charismatics take a very different tack in interpreting the healings and exorcisms of the Gospels. Unlike the dispensationalists, who say the miracles of New Testament times have a place in that dispensation but not in our dispensation, the charismatics see miracles as an ordinance of the church. Like the sacraments, they should be a continuing part of the Christian church's ministry. When MacArthur argues that the purpose of the miracles was to make it clear that Jesus was the Christ, he means we should not therefore expect this kind of healing ministry in the church today. It had its function in New Testament times but, since we have the inspired witness of Scripture today that is sufficient witness to establish both the true divinity and the true humanity of Christ, miracles are no longer necessary.

What is more than clear to me after listening to these sermons, is that those who can take the text the way it is, seem to make a lot more sense of it than those who are always trying to second-guess it. Surely one of the greatest strengths of MacArthur's preaching ministry is his complete confidence in the text.

Let us look for a brief moment at our preacher as an orator. One could evaluate his oratory very differently. My first impression is that he has little to offer from the standpoint of oratory. Listening to the tapes one has to say that he is the antithesis of Lloyd Ogilvie. Thinking about it a bit longer, however, I have to admit he does have techniques of getting people to listen that we should not overlook . . . He seems to have a feel for the use of rhythm in his preaching. Sometimes his rhythms are rapid and sometimes very slow. These pulpit rhythms, which we think of as being hopelessly old-fashioned . . . somehow make it possible for the listener to absorb and retain quite a bit of material over a long period of time. MacArthur's rhetoric is terribly out of date, but maybe he knows something the rest of us don't.

Why do so many people listen to MacArthur, this product of all the wrong schools? How can he pack out a church on Sunday morning in an age in which church attendance has seriously lagged. Here is a preacher who has nothing in the way of a winning personality, good looks, or charm. What he seems to have is a witness to true authority. He recognizes in Scripture the Word of God, and when he preaches, it is Scripture that one hears. It is not that the words of John MacArthur are so interesting as it is that the Word of God is of surpassing interest. That is why one listens.[2]

Had Old met MacArthur he would have had to revise one statement in the last paragraph! He has missed the point that the preacher at Grace Community Church deliberately seeks to keep a projection of his own personality out of the message.

[2] Hughes Oliphant Old, *The Reading and Preaching of the Scriptures in the Worship of the Christian Church, vol. 7, Our Own Time* (Grand Rapid: Eerdmans, 2010).

LIFE'S MOST IMPORTANT QUESTION

Introduction: Luke 9:18-22

read —

" WHO DO YOU SAY THAT I AM?"

W/ THAT QUESTION JESUS CONFRONTED HIS APOSTLES
W/ THE MOST CRITICAL ISSUE THEY WOULD EVER
FACE — OR YOU WILL EVER FACE — THE
QUESTION OF THE IDENTITY OF JESUS.

The answer to that question is not just
an issue that effects belief & lifestyle —
it effects one's eternal destiny.

ALL SOULS ON THIS PLANET IS ACCOUNTABLE
TO GOD FOR THEIR ANSWER TO THAT QUERY.
THE WRONG ANSWER OR NO DAMNS FOREVER!
THE RIGHT ANSWER OPENS THE DOOR TO
ETERNAL LIFE & JOY!

NOTE: Philosophers have answers, liberal
theologians have answers, false religions
have answers (mormons to JW's),
secularists have answers, atheists &
humanists have answers — SADLY,
THEY ARE WRONG OR UNCOMMITTED.

WHERE YOU SPEND YOUR ETERNITY
WILL BE DETERMINED BY HOW YOU
ANSWER THIS QUESTION & WHAT YOU
DO W/ THAT ANSWER —

24. First page of John's sermon notes on 'Life's Most Important
Question' from Luke 9:18-22. Page size here is reduced.

I should not leave the campus of Grace Church without adding a word on how it appears on a weekday. Even without the Sunday crowds the car park is far from empty and there is plenty of activity. Work is going on in all the offices which form a wing to the main auditorium. Across an open courtyard from the auditorium is the fine building opened in 1998 for the Master's Seminary, with four hundred currently in attendance. For the Seminary chapel the original chapel building to which MacArthur came in 1969 is used. On another part of the campus Grace Community School continues, with 260 pupils and fourteen staff under the headship of Tom Chaffin. One venue with a special draw for me is the Book Store, originally 'The Book Shack'. It is now a full-scale work, open all week, with shelves filled with books most likely to help the church and not necessarily the latest popular titles. Those attending Grace Church often hear from their pastor such words as the following:

> The role high-quality books play in our lives is absolutely critical. So why do so many Christians find it difficult to apply themselves to books? A. W. Tozer said that 'to enjoy a great religious book requires a degree of consecration to God and detachment from the world that few modern Christians have.' While it takes great determination to form new habits and cultivate our minds through books, even greater are the rewards you'll see in your thought patterns and your spiritual growth. When it comes to how we spend our spare moments, have we passively allowed the world to squeeze us into its mould? What can we do today to change that?

Before we leave the campus of Grace Community Church I will share a thought that inevitably comes to my mind on such visits. There is a likeness to the work of C. H. Spurgeon, who died in 1892, that cannot be missed. That is not because Sun Valley is any kind of imitation. I doubt if John MacArthur had very much acquaintance with Spurgeon's life and work until the 1980s when a great student of Spurgeon in the person of Phil Johnson came to join him. As should already be clear, the work of Grace Community Church developed without following any known example. Yet the resemblance is there, and it is because both men were given similar ambitions for the cause of Christ. Spurgeon gave priority to a college for preparing preachers and missionaries; organized conferences at which the spiritual growth of pastors was uppermost;[3] wrote and promoted Christian literature of the Puritan school; presided over a Society for the distribution of Christian literature; and never lost sight of the world as a mission field. MacArthur would be the last to draw a parallel, but it exists, and indeed extends beyond the features already mentioned. Both men loved young people: Spurgeon was the president of two Orphanages, and MacArthur of the Master's College.

What is certain is that MacArthur found in Spurgeon's fortitude and discernment a strengthening encouragement as the twentieth century came to its close; he saw him as a 'kindred spirit' although he hastened to add, 'I sit at his feet, not by his side.' He writes of how he stood at Spurgeon's grave one summer's day in London in 1992, and reflected on the similarity between the contemporary church situation and the dangers which 'thrust Spurgeon into a battle that ultimately led to his

---

[3] 'For real usefulness graces are better than gifts. As the man is, so is his work. If we would do better we must be better.' Such was Spurgeon's conviction, and it is also MacArthur's: 'A leader's effectiveness is always bound up in his character. It is the pastor's example that ultimately lends credibility to his message.'

death'.[4] With Spurgeon he dreaded an increased toleration of worldliness in the church:

'Many would like to unite church and stage, cards and prayer, dancing and sacraments. If we are powerless to stem this torrent, we can at least warn people of its existence, and entreat them to keep out of it. When the old faith is gone, and enthusiasm for the gospel is extinct, it is no wonder that people seek something else in the way of delight. Lacking bread, they feed on ashes.'

MacArthur quotes these words of Spurgeon's, but his own are very like them.

I judge that there is another similarity between these two men. At times it was a great burden for Spurgeon to realize not only that thousands looked for the help of his ministry, but that the very livelihood of Christian workers and missionaries, and the support of several agencies, all depended on his presence. If, on occasions, his friends saw him depressed, it was commonly in connection with this burden. John MacArthur would be less than human if he did not feel the same weight of responsibility, but any references to this are brief: 'Our ministry exacts a price – one that alone we could not bear.' He is sustained by a praying wife and people, and ultimately because he knows, as Spurgeon knew, that all lasting work is truly the work of God Himself. Christ's work will all be fulfilled, and it is in no way dependent on the instruments He chooses to employ. The text Susannah Spurgeon chose for her husband's 'Funeral Sermon', could not have been more suitable: 'For David after he had served his own generation by the will of God, fell on sleep' (*Acts* 13:36).[5] When the service of one man is done, the work of God is certain to go on.

[4] *Ashamed of the Gospel,* p. xi.
[5] *Metropolitan Tabernacle Pulpit,* vol. 38, 1892, pp. 73-84.

'Do you have any fear about the future of this ministry?' MacArthur was asked in recent years. To which he replied:

None whatsoever! God has supported it through times when we did not believe it could survive. God sustains what He wills, and we have seen His hand. My concern is to be a man of spiritual integrity, to have a ministry of spiritual integrity, and simply to teach the Bible under the promise that God blesses His own Word. To what extent He blesses, it fully satisfies me. I say this all the time, as long as God wants to sustain this ministry we will rejoice in that. And when He no longer needs it, we will rejoice in whatever other ministry takes its place.

25. Aerial photo of Grace Community Church Campus, courtesy of Lukas VanDyke.

25. Dr John MacArthur

17

The Man

*F*rom the above pages I believe the reader will have already formed an impression of John MacArthur as a man. Yet, as I said at the outset, these pages are little more than a sketch; this is not the time, nor I the writer, to give a full portrait.

I have heard members of Grace Community Church describe their pastor in a single sentence. An elder's wife, who has been there through the forty years, told me, 'We have a worshipper for a pastor.' Another believed, 'His greatest sermon is his life.' 'He is profoundly generous', commented a third. One of his longest-serving elders recalls how MacArthur never wants to discuss money at their meetings, unless it is to decline a rise in salary.

But before I conclude there are a few particular features on which I want to pause.

By temperament and by grace, diligence is evident in John MacArthur to an uncommon degree. Commitment to hard work marks his life. To the casual observer, the role he has been given in serving a large and supportive church might seem an enviable one. Behind that role, however, there is a weight of responsibility which few would sustain. If his burden was known, it is not one which others would readily take up. To remain joyful through forty years in the care of one congregation, and fresh in the constant preaching of the Word of God, is a demand human nature cannot sustain. It is grace that has kept his input from diminishing with the years. 'Our pastor gets better and better', can be heard at Sun Valley, as it was heard in Spurgeon's church when his youth was past.

But in addition to the church, John has the ultimate responsibility for all the young men involved in the Master's Seminary, and he also takes very seriously the trust which thousands of parents place in him when they send their young people to the Master's College. The work of these institutions, and of Grace to You, is never far from his thoughts. Their concerns are his concerns, and at times not without anxieties. He knows something of the feeling Paul expressed in the words, 'For now we live if you stand fast in the Lord' (*1 Thess.* 3:8).

In addition to this, there are the long hours spent alone on the preparation of the books that have served so many. Thirty hours a week in his study has remained normal. Without diligence all this would have been impossible. It is perseverance, conjoined with grace, that brings blessing. 'The plans of the diligent lead surely to abundance' (*Prov.* 21:5). 'Whoever sows sparingly will also reap sparingly, and whoever sows bountifully will also reap bountifully' (*2 Cor.* 9:6).

Connected with diligence, is a feature which Richard Mayhue has put among the first of his friend's characteristics. He says that MacArthur, whether in his desire to find out all he can on a text of Scripture, or in coveting information on many subjects, is driven by 'curiosity'. He wants to get to the bottom of everything. While this isn't a quality usually mentioned by those who advise on the Christian ministry, some have noticed it. Eugene Dolloff quotes the words, 'Curiosity is, in great and generous minds, the first passion and the last', and believed: 'God places a high rating on this human quality inbred in our very being.'[1]

No less prominent among MacArthur's features is the one which might seem incompatible with what has just been said. There is a calmness to his life which numbers have noted. In part this may be attributed to a genetic code that came uninterrupted from Scotland. Scots are not commonly excitable or outwardly emotional people. How much this enters into his temperament struck me when I heard a chairman interviewing him and John Piper together. MacArthur seemed almost incredulous at the way Piper could speak both of his elations and his depressions. Life for him was altogether more on a level.

If, however, he ever makes reference to his Scottish roots it is in a different context. Once for example, it came out when he was answering questions on Christian dress, and warning that dress codes should not be made tests of spirituality. Although he had liberty, he said, to wear controversial items, he would not do so out of consideration for his Christian testimony: 'I do not wear a skirt, but I want you to know that as a Scotchman, we have the right to do that. Kilts have been in our family for years.' No one has accused Scots of lacking in humour!

But the even temper of which I am speaking has more to do with grace than nature. Mrs Pat Rotisky, his personal secretary since 1986, says that she has never seen him angry, unless over

---

[1] Eugene D. Dolloff, *Maturing in the Ministry* (New York: Round Table, 1938), p. 168.

issues which concerned the honour of God. Emergencies do not fluster him, nor is he intimidated if confronted by anger or emotion. An intruder entering his office at the church, weapon in hand, and finding him alone, is quietly handled. At a parents' meeting connected with the church's High School, which MacArthur was chairing, a man lost his temper over a decision taken by the elders and spoke improperly. MacArthur quietly responded, 'We do not conduct meetings in this manner; this meeting is over.' Another time a man interrupted a Sunday service by walking down the aisle and ascending the pulpit platform; the pastor moved across to meet him with the words, 'Can I help you, brother?'

Richard Mayhue especially remembers the day he arrived in Los Angeles to stay with the MacArthurs for a week. It was the end of March 1980, and the *Los Angeles Times* had just broken the news that MacArthur and his church were to be prosecuted by the father of Ken Nally. As noted earlier, the impending court case potentially threatened the future of Grace Community Church, and the dramatic subject was the talk of the hour. Yet in Mayhue's week with MacArthur his host showed not the least concern about it.

There is another characteristic of MacArthur's personality which has been essential to his ministry, namely, his tenderness and graciousness in dealing with people. He does not hold himself aloof. That is not to say that, in a congregation of several thousand people, he is readily available to all. Were that the case his ministry could never have been sustained. He has safeguards against interruptions, and cannot simply pass the time of day with anyone who has time to talk. But every Sunday he is available at the front after the service to speak to all who wish; no one is left with problems unattended; and those who do speak with him are universally met with kindness and consideration. Despite the length of the queue below the pulpit, each individual has his full and patient attention.

This was a feature Tom Pennington, a former colleague, particularly remembered of his time at Grace Community Church:

> We overheard the conversations at the front of the church when you were dealing with those terribly confused—or, even worse, there to confront you or correct you. Or when some dear Christian was asking the same question he or she had heard you answer a dozen times before. And we watched you answer the question again and direct them to some resource—often at your own expense.

It is one of the most significant characteristics of MacArthur's ministry that, while he is involved in the wider work of Christ, his role as the pastor of the people entrusted to him remains a first priority and shapes his character. When questioned on a decrease of humour in his ministry, his brief comment revealed much: 'As a shepherd, you live with the pain of your people. You live with their disappointments. There is an accumulated sadness.'

In times of relaxation, away from crowds it is easier for MacArthur to socialize. Steve Esmond, who, with John, led a party in three coaches on the Reformation Tour in September 2006, noted how well the pastor got on with their German guide, and commented, 'He is a very likeable man, truly a gracious and humble servant of God.'

Tom Pennington once asked John, 'What's the biggest mistake leaders make?' He answered at once, 'That's easy—being impatient with people, not giving them time to grow.' In Pennington's eyes, John is a model of patience and forbearance. Addressing John at the dinner for former staff in 2009, he said:

> I remember one day in a pastoral staff meeting we were talking about a pastoral counselling situation and a man who had some significant issues in his life. You were sitting at the end of the conference table, reading and giving every appearance of being disengaged—which, of course, we had learned, you never were. And as so often happened, you spoke up, and interjected in our discussion, 'Everybody's got baggage. If you don't have baggage you're not going anywhere.'

John, seconded by Patricia, would be the first to say that his patience comes from grace and not from his nature.

As these pages should have made clear, Grace Community Church has a great many 'working' Christians. As one of his oldest elders emphasizes, 'John wants people to do the work.' But it is not organization that secures that result. It is love for the Saviour and love for the one who speaks in His name. Affection for the pastor marks the life of the church. Members understand it is impossible for him to be in all their homes, yet they also know he can be present when there is critical illness or special need. While other staff members have the regular responsibility of hospital visitation, there are times when they discover he has been there before them.

Our Lord puts 'Blessed are the poor in spirit' first among the Beatitudes. The trait has not always been prominent in evangelicalism. Tom Pennington, in speaking at the anniversary dinner already mentioned, said,

> I worked in Christian radio for twelve years and interacted with a number of other well-known teachers and Christian leaders. Tragically, there were plenty of occasions to see pride and self-promotion at their ugliest.

In contrast, referring to his years as an Associate Pastor beside John, he said,

> While we have not learned this well, in you we have at least learned what it looks like to be humble. You have routinely given the credit for your success to others. You don't like being the centre of attention. You have never sought or tolerated the role of *prima donna*.

In saying this, Pennington knew he was not praising his leader for an attainment. He has understood, with John, Christ's teaching. Humility is remembering what we are before God, owing everything to his grace: 'Humility is not a necessary human work to make us worthy, but a necessary divine work to make us see that we are unworthy and cannot change our condition before God.' 'The mark of a mature life is not sinlessness, which is reserved for heaven, but growing awareness of sinfulness.'[2] 'The believer sees himself before God: poor, sorrowful, meek, hungry.'[3] The Christian ought to have no problem in seeing that Paul was not referring to a former condition and a past experience when he speaks of himself as a 'wretched man'.

---

[2] *MacArthur New Testament Commentary Matthew 1-7*, pp. 149, 160.
[3] *The Jesus You Can't Ignore*, p. 132. This comment is on the leading beatitudes (*Matt.* 5:3-6). 'Jesus could hardly have devised a list of virtues more at odds with His culture.'

Paul wrote those words at the height of his ministry. Yet righteousness and sin were still fighting a battle in his life. As he acknowledges in Romans 7:25, the way of victory is 'through Jesus Christ our Lord', but the rest of the verse makes clear that, at that time, the victory was not yet complete. Permanent victory is assured to us now, but it is not given to us now.

It is the practical consequences of humility that are visible. In MacArthur it includes willingness to esteem others, and to listen to opinions that differ from his own. While he preaches with boldness and certainty, in his personal life he has no air of infallibility and knows that such an attitude cannot consist with 'lowliness of mind'. With all Christians, he remains a pupil in the school of Christ. He writes:

> The fruits of true, Christlike leadership are humility, tenderness, self-sacrifice, and affection for the sheep. A good shepherd embodies what every leader in the church should strive to be: personal, patient, gentle, hands-on, and self-giving . . . Overbearing autocrats who seem incapable of empathy or kindness are not fit leaders at all. The key to effective leadership has very little to do with wielding authority and much to do with giving oneself.[4]

Pennington gives the following story of something that happened on one occasion when he was travelling with John and Patricia for a preaching service in Denver. On arriving at the airport it was necessary to hire a car to take them to the church. But no vehicle was available other than an expensive Cadillac. With no alternative, they were obliged to take it.

---

[4] 'The Pastor as Leader' in *For the Fame of God's Name, Essays in Honor of John Piper* (Wheaton: Crossway, 2010), pp. 465, 469.

You were so concerned about the message that it would send, and it was so contrary to your nature, that you stopped the car several blocks from the church. And you, Patricia, and I walked the rest of the way to the church in the cold. I'm sure the people that night wondered why the MacArthurs were walking to church.

That same characteristic enters into his acceptance of speaking engagements. Accustomed to addressing large numbers, the size of the number does not determine where he will speak. Thanking him for a visit, an organizer of a Christian camp wrote to him: 'I want to express my total appreciation of your willingness to come and share with our small crowd at Hume Lake. The reactions were excellent and I know God fed many hearts.'[5] That letter was written in 1979, but it has remained his practice, as some of us saw a few years ago when a comparatively small conference of young people at Leicester, England, were thankful to have him with them for a whole weekend.

What humility means for MacArthur brings us back to the fundamental principle of his ministry: all success lies in the Word of God. He can admire such servants of Christ as Luther and Spurgeon, yet at once he would add: 'It's not the man, it's the truth of God and the power of God in the man.' Those who have sat under John MacArthur's ministry have been taught the same lesson. Thirty years after Grace to You was launched, Jay Flowers, a staff member, concluded an article on the work with the testimony:

Our current level of ministry seemed impossible in 1969. In human terms, it was. What we have seen happen during

---

[5] Ken Poure, July 27, 1979.

our first thirty years is no monument to John MacArthur, our staff, or our ingenuity, but to God's faithfulness to bless His Word.[6]

As with all leaders, natural gifts enter into what John MacArthur is, but these alone would be no explanation of his life. Words he spoke to ministers in 1997 go to the heart of things:

> The greatest privilege of my ministry that I have, is not the time I spend with people, it is the time I get to spend with *Him*. And the cultivation of the knowledge of Him in the study of the Word of God, and prayer and meditation, is the heart and soul of my life and the greatest joy of ministry for me. Whatever may happen out there, or might not happen out there, whatever changes or doesn't change, whatever disappoints or encourages, the Lord never changes; and it is in His love that I find the constancy for my life, the strength for ministry, and the joy as well.

These words explain the enduring priority of John MacArthur's life and the priority he has constantly brought before others. He started a Grace to You letter in June 2009 with the question, 'What sermon would you want to preach to a chapel service for thousands of military cadets of all faiths?' From the above pages we should be able to anticipate what his own answer would be when he had that opportunity. At a Sunday chapel service at the U.S. Military Academy at West Point a tradition has been observed for more than a hundred years that the new class of freshmen cadets each receive a personalized Bible. Invited to preach at a Sunday service at West Point where this would happen, John later commented, 'I taught from Psalm 19—a

---

[6] Article 'Mission Impossible' in *Grace Today*, February 28, 1999.

favourite of mine—on "The Power and Sufficiency of God's Word".' Facing men among whom some would soon be seeing death in combat situations, he spoke of the Book through which God changes the lives of all who truly listen.

As a young man John MacArthur made a commitment to study the Word of God. He had no idea then what that commitment would mean, but he looks back on it now as 'the most profound choice I ever made'. It led him to the proclamation which can affirm, 'We believe, and therefore speak' (*2 Cor.* 4:13). From this came the shepherding of the people of God and a personal life of trust in God. He has taught that the sufficiency of Scripture means that no situation can arise in which its light is not relevant. No need is unmet where its directions and promises are followed. 'All flesh is as grass, and all the glory of man as the flower of grass. But the word of the Lord endures forever' (*1 Pet.* 1:24, 35). If we were to ask the pastor of Grace Church for a last word, I believe it could be this:

> God's Word is bold, honest, and direct, cutting across the grain of popular culture. It penetrates hearts, illuminates minds, and transforms lives. Our circumstances and preferences don't inform or liven up the Bible, dictate its meaning, or determine how it applies to our lives. It is eternal truth, living and active, and it cuts to the heart of every issue. Its meaning is fixed, and applicable to everyone, everywhere. Scripture speaks with absolute authority as it guides believers, confronts error, and brings clarity to even the most confusing theological questions.

There's simply no substitute for Scripture. Nothing else is as trustworthy and steadfast as the Word of God. Church tradition changes over time. Authors and pastors make mistakes. Even your own conscience can be wrong. All believers must be like the Bereans Paul describes in Acts 17:11, measuring everything we hear, read, and see against the perfect, unchanging standard of the Bible. The authority and power of God's Word is unmistakeable and unforgettable.[7]

So it will be in all generations. What William Cowper wrote three centuries ago will be the experience of all Christians until time is no more.

> The Spirit breathes upon the Word,
> And brings the truth to sight:
> Precepts and promises afford
> A sanctifying light.
>
> The hand that gave it still supplies
> The gracious light and heat;
> His truths upon the nations rise;
> They rise, but never set.
>
> Let everlasting thanks be Thine
> For such a bright display,
> As makes a world of darkness shine
> With beams of heavenly day.
>
> My soul rejoices to pursue
> The steps of Him I love,
> Till glory breaks upon my view
> In brighter worlds above.

---

[7] Grace to You letter of August, 2010.

Index

OTHER CURRENT TITLES BY
IAIN H. MURRAY
PUBLISHED BY
THE BANNER OF TRUTH TRUST

The Banner of Truth Trust originated in 1957 in London. The founders believed that much of the best literature of historic Christianity had been allowed to fall into oblivion and that, under God, its recovery could well lead not only to a strengthening of the church today but to true revival.

Inter-denominational in vision, this publishing work is now international, and our lists include a number of contemporary authors along together with classics from the past. The translation of these books into many languages is encouraged.

A monthly magazine, *The Banner of Truth,* is also published and further information will be gladly supplied by either of the offices below.

3 Murrayfield Road, Edinburgh, EH12 6EL, UK
PO Box 621, Carlisle, Pennsylvania 17013, USA
www.banneroftruth.co.uk

EVANGELICALISM DIVIDED
A Record of Crucial Change in the years 1950 to 2000
ISBN–13: 978 0 85151 783 4,
Hardback, 352 pp.

'Iain Murray's historical overview of the fortunes and misfortunes of evangelical Christianity, especially in England, between 1950 and the century's endtime, will stir up both an approving and a dissenting readership. But no one can contend that it ignores some of the most vital theological issues of the time and the conflicts surrounding them. The narrative is well documented, and it details not only conflicts of perspective but inconsistencies and alterations of views in some of the leading participants in the events of the day.'

CARL F. H. HENRY

PENTECOST TODAY
The Biblical Basis for Understanding Revival
ISBN–13: 978 0 85151 752 0
Hardback, 242 pp.

'If you only ever read one book on revival – and all serious Christians should read at least one – read this one. Drawing on a wealth of pastoral wisdom, an almost unrivalled grasp of the history of God's people in these islands and a thorough working knowledge of the Puritans, Iain Murray is well place to give a definitive statement of the biblical basis for revival. The fanatic and the sceptic and all shades between will be challenged and helped by the clear presentation found here.'

GRACE MAGAZINE

LLOYD-JONES: MESSENGER OF GRACE
ISBN–13: 978 0 85151 975 3
Hardback, 288 pp.

CHAPTERS: The Lloyd-Jones Legacies; Preaching and the Holy Spirit; The Evangelical Use of the Old Testament; Skeletons in the Cupboard; Raising the Standard of Preaching; Lloyd-Jones and Spurgeon Compared; A Controversial Book, *Joy Unspeakable;* 'The Lost Leader' or 'A Prophetic Voice'?; The End of the Puritan Conference; Some Convictions of Lloyd-Jones in Miniature; Inventory of Lloyd-Jones's Sermons; An Analysis of the Sermons on Ephesians; *Is the Reformation Over?* A Review.

This is not a repetition of material in Murray's two-volume biography of Lloyd-Jones; it concentrates on three main themes in his thought and ministry, and includes much unpublished material.

THE OLD EVANGELICALISM
Old Truths for a New Awakening
ISBN–13: 978 0 85151 901 2
Hardback, 226 pp.

CHAPTERS: Preaching and Awakening: Facing the Main Problem in Evangelism; Spurgeon and True Concersion; 'Christ our Righteousness' – God's Way of Salvation; The Cross – The Pulpit of God's Love; What Can We Learn from John Wesley?; Assurance of Salvation; Christian Unity and Church Unity.

'There is much to stimulate us to godliness in this volume. I thank God for Iain Murray's fifty years of service to the church and the influence of his books for posterity.'

MARK R. BROWN, NEW HORIZONS

HEROES
ISBN–13: 978 1 84871 024 5
Hardback, 320 pp.

'The reviewer found these lessons edifying, instructive, challenging and encouraging. We heartily agree with the author's dictum: 'The study of history is vital to the health of the Church.' The book is an excellent holiday companion and a good fireside read. It is heartily recommended.'

DONALD MACDONALD, THE RECORD

THE UNDERCOVER REVOLUTION
How Fiction Changed Britain
ISBN–13: 978 1 84871 012 2
Paperback, 112 pp.

W. R. Inge, writing in the first half of the twentieth century predicted what kind of nation would come into being if the outlook of many of the modern novelists was allowed to change British culture: 'No God. No country. No family. Refusal to serve in war. Free love. More play. Less work. No punishments. Go as you please. It is difficult to imagine any programme which, if carried out, would be more utterly ruinous to a country situated as Great Britain is today.'

'Iain Murray has put his finger on the turning point that sent western culture down the path of immorality. It is a persuasive explanation that we need to hear.'

JOHN MACARTHUR

A SCOTTISH CHRISTIAN HERITAGE
ISBN–13: 978 0 85151 930 2
Hardback, 416 pp.

'Informative, challenging and encouraging, this survey of the spiritual inheritance of Scotland provided an invaluable three-part introduction to Scottish Church History. It first introduces significant individuals. The second part illustrates the contribution the Church of Scotland has made to missionary enterprise, and the third deals with four Church issues.'

DEREK PRIME, LIFE AND WORK

WESLEY AND MEN WHO FOLLOWED
ISBN–13: 978 0 85151 835 0
Hardback, 288 pp.

Leading Calvinists of the nineteenth century, such as J. C. Ryle and C. H. Spurgeon, who stood closer to the blessings of the eighteenth century revival, were admirers of Wesley. In William Cunningham's *British and Foreign Evangelical Review*, it was said of Wesleyan Methodists, 'With all their errors of opinion, and all their faults of administration, they have done more for the propagation of the gospel at home and abroad, in England and America, and among the heathen, than any other sect at present existing.' Yet too many present-day Calvinists have supposed there is nothing important for us to learn from Wesley and leading evangelists who followed him. Murray has found much value in knowing them.

A DAY'S MARCH NEARER HOME
AUTOBIOGRAPHY OF J. GRAHAM MILLER
Edited by Iain H. Murray
ISBN–13: 978 1 84871 064 1
Hardback, 352 pp.

This book will surely endure as one of the few outstanding Christian autobiographies of the twentieth century. Graham Miller, lawyer, missionary, pastor and preacher, did not write for publication. But certain of the value of his autobiographical records, Iain Murray edited his friend's material after his death, counting it a high privilege to do so. Dr Miller was a man so much loved that the nation of Vanuatu held a day of national mourning when his full life of ninety-four years came to an end. The title 'A Day's March Nearer Home' comes from a favourite hymn learned in his youth in New Zealand. While likely to be of special interest to ministers and missionaries, there is much here to appeal to all.